Table of Contents

TABOOS

Pedophilia and Necrophilia: Christian research perspective

A comparative study of the impact of spiritual transformation through Christian education, as well as the South African tax payer's outcry of why criminals should have free education. A book that explores recidivism through education support and advocacy, with the underlying taboo crimes: Pedophilia and Necrophilia.

This book is well researched and can be used by students studying criminology, psychology, philosophy, police academy, prison ministry, justice systems, prison environments and human trafficking educational institutions.

Dr. Rev. Val Hamann (Ph.D.) © 2022

ACKNOWLEDGEMENTS

I dedicate this book to my parents Roy Dudley and Priscilla Eileen Webster, who support all my endeavours. My dedication expands to my three children Taryn, Jessica and Brandon.

My research and knowledge has been greatly influenced by my experience in prisons as a prison ministry leader for fourteen years, where I have taught faith based programs in nine different prisons, conducted pastoral care counselling to offenders and written eight books to assist offenders throughout South Africa. Thank you to each person: Pastors, Offenders, Ex-Offenders, Prison Ministry Leaders, Prison Ministry Organisation Representatives and Prison Authorities that I was able to interview in person. Your perspectives, information and insights are invaluable and much appreciated.

I pray for paedophiles, child traffickers and necrophiles worldwide, that they will be exposed to the truth that Christ Jesus saves from the path of destruction they are headed towards if they choose to remain without him. I pray that God's kindness will lead them to repentance. I pray that victims of paedophiles and traffickers, will experience God's protection, saving power, healing and comfort through the Holy Spirit, in addition to restoration through the blood of Jesus.

TENTATIVE STATEMENT OF THE PROBLEM

This book centers on the intersections of recidivism measurements, comparing the South African taxpayer's negative outcry of why free education in prisons remains available to the incarcerated, while it has no positive impact on recidivism as inmates do not desire to change. The taxpayer prefers the 'lock them up and throw away the key' approach, while the church responds, 'Jesus is the key that sets them free.'

The church's reaction illuminates that education as the pursuit of knowledge is a basic human right and the Christian educational approach, encourages spiritual transformation. Christian education offers a model of non-judgmental love and justice, as a corrective measure, which focuses on the reduction of recidivism and supports rehabilitation, which includes lack of opportunities for ex-inmates to obtaining employment. The high rate of crime and overcrowding in prisons in South Africa, motivated this study.

Christian educational healing programs for sexual crimes are in place and utilized in prisons, but none defend the topics specifically for necrophilia and pedophilia.

RESEARCH

Based on the argument of Christian education impacting the recidivism and rehabilitation rates, to clarify, I examine the effects of spiritual transformation, through research, interviewing relevant candidates, surveys, statistics and facts, describing the strong and vulnerable points of the incarcerated people's rights in an oppressive environment and evaluate the taxpayer's outcry, helping them find an amicable structure of liberatory conclusions, through writing that is both redemptive and communal.

I examine what pedophilia and necrophilia which is often related to child marital rape (child brides), cults and incest.

EXPLORING SOLUTIONS

Prison ministries offer a wide scope of rehabilitation programs that are extensively used throughout the world. Some famous programs include Restorative Justice, Fatherhood, Crossroads, Kairos International and Prison Fellowship International, Church Leadership and Ministry Development, HIV and Aids Programs, NICRO (National Institute for Crime Prevention and the Reintegration of Offenders) as well as the Prison Yoga Project.

Although there are programs to assist sex offenders, they focus more on rape and not on assisting inmates whose crimes are related to pedophilia and necrophilia. Kingdom diversity initiative is a central component throughout the world of prison ministries and educational programs, responding to fulfill the 'Great Commission.'

There are however, many different denominations represented through prison ministry leaders, pastors and teachers with different statements of faith, cultural backgrounds and belief systems that are given access by the prison chaplains, to minister to and educate inmates. These diverse systems frequently cause confusion and oppression, rather than liberation for the inmates, through the varied pluralistic knowledge and sentiments that they obtain. While Yoga would raise eyebrows among Christians, non-Christians would relish the relaxation techniques.

However, the point remains, the taxpayer's outrage of funding any 'projects' for a society of offenders that they deem unfit and undeserving of receiving anything good, based on the bad choices they made in the past.

Faith based educational programs in prisons seem to lack the depth that higher education offers. While promoting God awareness and redemptive biblical knowledge, Christian education deprives the prisoner of political, financial, mathematical, medical, scientific, skills development, employment readiness and life skills knowledge.

This book is mainly based on the South African vantage point, but not limited to, will highlight influences from all perspectives, bridging the gap between the diverse opinions and biblical foundation conclusions.

The underlying crime of choice for this book will focus on pedophilia which includes child trafficking and necrophilia, the study of which would assist the reader to make their own conclusive assessments. Even after years of research, pedophilia and necrophilia is not yet determined as a mental illness nor sexual orientation. This book will test the theory that Christian education deters pedophile and necrophile inmates from practicing as such, rehabilitates them, reduces recidivism or makes no impact at all.

Becoming a Christian proves difficult for some people, as it is not measured by what they gain (Jesus Christ, redemption, grace, salvation, eternal life) but rather by what would they need to give up (sexual sin, smoking, drinking, gambling and such).

Determining what role of sexual element was played in a killing and determining if a killing was sexually motivated, is a difficult task as any killing that is not easily identifiable, is recorded as 'motive unknown' (Folino: 2000). Each killing is unique and there is no common agreement or full understanding on necrophilia behaviour, which is necessary to explore if we are to progress in detection, research, assessment and supportive treatment.

There are few studies that apply experimental and pragmatic methods to faith based programs to determine how effective they are. Faith based programs also have a reputation from critics for 'forcing' religious beliefs onto inmates, violating their rights. Advocates credit Christian education with providing life-changing behavioural patterns, improved morality and learning experiences on offenders who desist from criminal activity.

Chapter 1   INTRODUCTION

I acquired an abundance of knowledge through this process of research on topics close to my heart, such as sentencing structures and rehabilitation of offenders, second chances, solitary confinement, recidivism, Gender Based Violence and Victim Empowerment (GBV & VE) as well as the study of offenders that have little or no assistance in their area of their offences. The offences of choice for this book, are based on necrophilia and pedophilia. My research has only scratched the surface of this multidimensional 'dark world' of sex crimes against humanity. Counselling paedophiles over the years has helped me tremendously to understand them, not judge them. It has been a difficult journey for me to not get emotionally affected by the crimes I have researched, with regards to the suffering of the victims that have been sexually abused in some way or another.[1]

When most people hear about someone practising pedophilia or necrophilia, their first response is usually:

- they should rot in hell
- they should be removed from civilisation
- they are monsters
- they are sex-pests
- they are sick and have no conscience
- they are violent and have no remorse
- they are perverts

---

[1] See Pages 63 and 64 of this book, research on torture of children on the Dark Web.

- they deserve to be castrated
- they are outcasts

It was only in the late 19th Century that pedophilia was named and formally recognised.

Although these sexual orientations are mostly directed at men, there are women who also exhibit this disorder. Besides the sexual attraction to children, they do not feel emotionally attached to them. In many cases, they kill the children after they have molested them and the men often have sex with the child's corpse. In the case of the child being left to live, they have a permanent stigma of stolen innocence. Paedophiles can also be necrophiles and visa-versa.

To date, no cure has been found to assist and it seems to be correlated with various neurological and psychological pathologies. There is no known exact cause either, it could possibly be from being abused as a child, but not necessarily. These conditions are the most stigmatised disorders and should non-practising paedophiles and necrophiles be judged, without committing any crime, they will refrain from seeking help and sink into depression. These 'conditions' are no respecter of a person's age, culture, background, race or social standing.

This book will explore the effects or absence of effect that Christian education has on offender's rehabilitation and spiritual transformation and the reduction of recidivism, in particular offender of the crimes pedophilia and necrophilia.

The crime rate in South Africa is high, which is a major concern and causes fear, resulting in some communities members of society to take the law into their own hands. South Africans are seeking solutions.

All education in prisons should encourage the offenders to be better people, not better criminals.

There is a butterfly effect to pedophilia and necrophilia, in that the detrimental choices made by just one man can shake a nation. And yet, there is a positive butterfly effect that can emerge, from the tragedy thereof.

Chapter 2   HISTORY AND BACKGROUND

2.1 The history of prison secular education that has influenced its theory and practice.

In the early 19th Century offenders were given religious instruction by chaplains, although secular programs were developed before Christian programs. Christian educational programs were developed to help offenders read bibles. The first important program developed for rehabilitating prisoners, was launched in 1876. The first survey pertaining to prisons took place in 1931, by Austin MacCormick, resulted in a book he wrote called: The Education of Adult Prisoners: A Survey and a Program. The book presents theories and their application thereof, to offender learners. The barriers to learning at that time, was untrained and lack of training for prison teachers, having practical programs in place and standards of practise. These three issues led MacCormick to found the Correctional Educational Association (CEA).[2]

A study was conducted in Nigerian prisons, sampling 190 offenders and 20 facilitators, to evaluate the effects of religious and philosophy education, as a way of uplifting offenders and curtailing ex-offenders recidivism rates. Results showed that religious education elevates the image of offenders and increases their capacity to change the course of their

---

[2] https://ceanational.org/conferences/ downloaded March 2021, depicts that the CEA still runs today, holding an annual conference in the USA.

lives. The recommendations that stemmed from the survey include prisons focusing on the development of the whole person, considering their psychological, economic, social and cultural backgrounds. Prison institutions were established in Nigeria in 1872 with the ultimate aims of offenders caught up in the warped justice system, to receive punishment such as whipping, banishment and death.[3] A government white paper detailed the functions of prison services as custody, diagnosis, correction, training and rehabilitation of offenders.[4] This meant that prisoners had to be treated with humanity and have assistance from institutions to lead law abiding worthwhile lives after their release. The two main points being: humanity and education in prisons.

In 1981, the African Charter on Human Rights (ACHR), adopted two forces, Organisation of African Unity (OAU) and African Union (AU). In 1986, they declared in Article 17 that 'every individual shall have the right to education,' as well as 'the freedom to take part in cultural life of the community,' which means that offenders have the same right to education as other citizens do. (Hawley et al: 2013) defines that this includes:

---

[3] Mango: 2006.
[4] Evawoma-Enuku: 2006.

- Education and training could reduce the cost of crime.
  (The costs of prisoners reoffending forms a large part of the cost of crime).
- Employment is a key factor in reducing the cost and risk of reoffending.
  (Recidivism is reduced when employment opportunities are presented).
- Prisons should assist offender with skills, knowledge and competencies.
  (Skills, knowledge and competencies assist with reintegration and rehabilitation).
- Prison should be an environment for positive behavioural and attitude changes.
  (Enhancing human dignity and presenting second {and more} chances).
- Education in prison provides a source of confidence and aspirations for the future.
  (Fundamental life and social skills, spiritual growth and transformation, help offenders cope with challenges and temptations they face outside of prison).

The first two prisons built in South Africa, were Malmesbury and Goodwood correctional services in the Western Cape. (Bruyns, Jonkers and Luyt 2007:6) state that in December 1997 Malmesbury was opened. It is the only prison in South Africa that consists of only single cells, which can house two prisoners at a time. Malmesbury can house 1330 prisoners in total, yet has a small staff compliment of 22 officials. It was architecturally designed and built different to other traditional prisons, as smaller units to house smaller groups of offenders, as a manner of better controlling them.

Other prisons house larger clusters, which are not always manageable and prove very challenging to keep it a safe environment, as offenders all come from different culture backgrounds, different religions and different levels of maturity, as well as being convicted for different levels of crimes.

All other prisons in South Africa were built in a way that offenders share rooms of up to 20 or more offenders per room. The notorious Pollsmoor prison is the largest prison in South Africa, housing 8,500 offenders at any given time. We are not to forget Robben Island, where people were almost totally banished from society. There are 243 prisons in South Africa, of these only 8 are for women.

The central theme for all prisons is the promotion of prisons as correctional facilities and the development of prisons into institutions of rehabilitation.[5] Positive manipulation of the prison environment, will contribute towards improved behaviour patterns of offenders.

In some countries, alternative penal reform alternatives have been explored and instituted, keeping the community safe and satisfying their requirements for retribution, while keeping offenders with lesser

---

[5] This theme is embedded in the Department's mandate in terms of Chapter 2, Section 36 (1) of the Constitution of the Republic of South Africa, as well as the Correctional Services Act 111 of 1998.

crime level sentencing, out of prisons. Four of these options are correctional supervision, parole supervision and two very rare occurrences – a prison that gives offenders their own keys, where offenders live with certain privileges, however if they do not abide by the rules they go back into the normal penal system. The other prison is in the USA where the doors never get locked! This prison is so isolated and anyone wanting to escape stands the risk of dying in the dessert sun, or being eaten by wild animals.

The Economic and Social Council (ESC) adopted significant new resolutions in May 1990, on prison education, training and public awareness in the crime prevention field. The council affirmed offender's rights to education.

Key indicators of the recommendations and considerations made in the resolutions are as follows:

- Provide various types of education that would contribute towards recidivism and crime prevention and reintegration
- The increased use of alternatives to imprisonment
- Education to be designed to develop the whole person, social, economic and cultural backgrounds
- All prisoners should have access to education, including literacy, vocational, religious, sports, cultural activities, library facilities and higher education

- Every effort should be made to coax prisoners to be recipients of education in all forms
- All authorities of prisons should facilitate and support educational opportunities for prisoners
- Formal educational opportunities should not be avoided
- Where possible, prisoners should be encouraged to partake in education outside of prison
- The necessary teaching staff , equipment and funding should be made available by the prison for the prisoners to receive suitable education

Education is deemed one of the means of furthering resocialisation of the skills that may assist prisoners build a better future, once released. Many prisoners initially participate in educational programs, for non-educational reasons, such as time out of their prison cells, being with friends, using the opportunity to move contraband or to see if there are teachers of the opposite sex that they can gaze at.

In South Africa between 1652 and 1980 Jan van Riebeeck described prisons as harsh and severe penalties with little provision for the spiritual needs of prisoners. In 1770 doors were opened by authorities to give churches free access to minister to their members and adherents in prison, which also reflected positively upon the future of prison ministry run in South Africa (Van Deventer: 1986: 3).

2.2 History of South African icon Nelson Mandela, impact of prison education.

Poem dedicated to Nelson Mandela Prisoner No: 46664:

The view of Table Mountain
For years, Madiba's only consolation
If only he had wings to fly
To promote the freedom cry!

Democracy united
A nation once divided
God sees all the pain
Of a land crying in vain

As boundaries come down
Refuse to wear the hate crown
That causes all the sorrow
Let's build a new tomorrow![6]

Nelson Mandela, born on 18 July 1918, was arrested and incarcerated from 1962 at Pollsmoor Prison in Cape Town, then Robben Island[7] - and finally released in 1990 from Drakenstein Prison in Paarl. He spent over 27 years in prison as a political 'resistance' offender. He won the Nobel Peace Prize in 1993 and won the presidential election in 1994, South Africa's first

---

[6] Excerpts of Poem called: Wild Dandelions, written by Val Hamann, dedication to Nelson Mandela in prison Robben Island, from the book My Pledge: Committed to Change, Published by Biblecor, 2016, Page 8.

[7] Robben Island, seven kilometres off the coast of Cape Town (sizing 3.3 Kilometres long and 1.9 Kilometres wide), a place of banishment and imprisonment, primarily for political prisoners.

democratically elected President. He won the hearts of the South African people and the whole country mourned his death. His legacy continues to live on as we celebrate Nelson Mandela 'Madiba's Day' where almost every citizen ad organisation partakes in 67 minutes of 'doing good' for those less fortunate. His famous prison number 466/64 is used as a fashion icon throughout the South African fashion world, printed on shoes, clothing and accessories, which was designed by Mr Herman Pillay, Chief Executive Officer at the famous fashion franchise Wear South African (Pty) Limited in Epping, part of the South African Clothing and Textile Workers Union (SACTWU), Cape Town. A famous movie actor, Danny Glover flew to South Africa from the USA, to promote Nelson Mandela's clothing line and managed to raise millions in funding during this campaign, to save the textile industry.

Nelson Mandela was studying law prior to his arrest, but failed three times, due to political problems and not being able to focus on his studies. When he arrived at Pollsmoor Prison, he finally had the chance to concentrate, especially when he was alone and knew he would pass, but unfortunately abandoned it. In his book called, 'Nelson Mandela: Conversations with myself' he records from his diary in prison that on 12 December 1984 his report stated that he failed all six subjects. He carefully noted that the number of prisoners who are studying in prison, in May 1978 were 334, of which 127 were completing their matric and 59 obtaining a degree. He also recorded that 30% of the total students, did not sit for the examination.[8] In 1989 he finally graduated with a LLB Degree through the University of South Africa, at the age of 71, just one year before his release. Although the opportunity presented itself to him, he never took it for the first 26 years of his incarceration.[9]

With 334 offenders studying at one prison in 1978, one must realise there was value in education for them, benefitting offender and prison.

2.3 The history of prison Christian education, as well as theological and philosophical underpinnings that have influenced its theory and practice.

The normal good values taught in households are often not held up in society, especially among the youth of today, which causes a breakdown of moral fibre. To correct this, correctional and developmental programs are presented.

Parole supervision is a service rendered by the Department of Correctional Services, however the shared responsibility also lays with the community. Parolees are given the opportunity to develop themselves in their own communities, in conjunction with other role players for the enhancement of the ex-offender's rehabilitation. The Department of

---

[8] Nelson Mandela: Conversations with Myself, book published by Macmillan © 2010 by the Nelson Mandela Foundation, Page 257, 279, 293. 306 and 415.

Correctional Services relies on half way houses, community and church members and faith based organisations to assist in the ex-offender with their spiritual growth, adaptation of their surroundings and overcoming challenges, employment opportunities, mentoring, support groups and safe accommodation. Coupled with this, Christian educational programs. These, among other means of support, are crucial to the ex-offender's success rate.

In Christianity, necrophilia was considered by the Catholic Church to be neither whoring 'fornication' nor brutishness, yet 'contamination with a propensity to whoring.'

According to Ulrich Lottering, Managing Director of Networking for Christ, 'It is very rare that a necrophile will become a gang member, as they are usually criminally profiled as 'loners.' Paedophiles are usually shunned completely by the prison population and often killed at the first opportunity offenders get, so paedophiles have to have special protection in prisons. A necrophile and paedophile will show no interest in attending Christian or secular programs, as they fear rejection from other offenders attending the same. If a support group can be established with a specific program addressing their crimes only, they will be more likely to want to attend. On the other hand, one solution to this particular problem could be to house all necrophiles and paedophiles in one central prison, where such programs can be run with more effective modus operandi and less judgement.'[10]

2.4 The major tenants of the purpose and scope of Christian education

Noah Webster, a biblical scholar, defined education as, Quote~ *'Comprehends all that series of instruction and discipline which is intended to enlighten the understanding, correct the temper, for the manners and habits of youth and fit them for usefulness in their future stations.'* The Apostle Paul also added his value and authenticity to God's word as, *'All scripture is inspired by God and is useful for correction, teaching reproof, training in righteousness, so that man can be found adequate and equipped for every good work,'* (2 Timothy 3: 16-17).

These two revelations define the heart of Christian education, from the foundations of theology and philosophy.

Furthermore, Christian education has always provided truth and exposure to:

- Development of a biblical worldview
- Christian character formation, spiritual maturity
- Academic excellence is a form of worship
- Mastery of the topic, core subject curriculum
- Learn to impart, teach methodology

---

[10] Managing Director of Networking for Christ SA, Ulrich Lottering interviewed on 5 April 2021.

- Historical knowledge foundational
- Knowledge and revelation of the Word of God
- Promotes sound, logical reasoning and intuitive thinking
- Applying biblical principles to everyday life
- Opportunities for personal spiritual growth and transformation
- Training up disciples
- Physical well being
- Godly behaviour patterns and discipline
- Promotes fear of the Lord and respect for authority

Briefly, all Christian education is rooted in Judaism and it is only possible to understand it by reverting back to its Jewish roots. The Old Testament began with God as teacher and instructor. The Christian life had an all-encompassing stimulus on many aspects of society as a whole, including politics, religions, family, law, calendars, languages, art and music, since its inception.

2.5 Religion, Education, Revolution.

Revolution, education and religion share a common destiny: they focus on the future of the youth and their natural demand to transform life for the good. As early as 1541 Calvin publicised his preoccupation with higher education when he announced in his Ecclesiastical Ordinances, 'we need to found a college for the instruction of those young people who are to be prepared for ministry and for civil government

(Pettegree, Duke and Lewis 1996: 36). Most of the towns had a black-out on leadership in the religious communities which consequently resulted in poor, unskilled and uneducated people groups being bereft, of the crucial leaders they needed. This left a void in the church, schools and civil government and also posed a risk to their future plans. Although the young were passionate, loyal and committed, they were still untrained and inexperienced. Calvin realised he needed to train ministers and if such a plan failed, people would turn back to the flesh of the pots of Egypt (an era of depression and slavery), instead of gravitating towards the land of milk and honey of Canaan (freedom, self-rule, abundance and security).

An ideal world would mean a greener world, where wealth is shared and opportunities are equal, fighting is non-existent and dealing with conflict without litigation and warfare. A world where healing the sick does not depend on the depth of their bank account and where respect is the norm, not the rare gem as it is today. There would be no crime, no poverty and unemployment and no divorce.

The most essential challenge is to create a better world for the future, today. Only education will bring this revolution.[11]

---

[11] Living Theology, Editors Len Hansen, Nico Koopman and Robert Vosloo, Published by Bible Media © 2013 Pages 601-606 written by H. Russel Botman.

Rehabilitation programs are only effective if the offender applies to their lives what they have learned, yet there are society taxpayers who believe Christian education has no effect. Based on research conducted by (Osmer: 2008) there is ample proof that religious rehabilitation programs have a positive effect on offenders and his practical theological interpretation method explored recidivism.

(Sphere: 2005: 37-47) Burl Cain, an offender in Angola knew that the public were afraid of offenders and their attitudes toward them, but he vowed to change their perception and surrounded himself with a team of offenders to create a new and improved prison. He knew more could be done in prison, to bring stability, reduce gang fights and change the mentality of 'every man for himself' to 'every man for God.' Through this process, the Angola prison achieved accreditation from the American Correctional Association (ACA) and has since maintained it. This accreditation identifies and is recognised as an entity that is safe, stable and constitutional. The turnaround of receiving Christian education was phenomenal, the success rate high and the recidivism rate minimal.

To further drive this point, it is believed that family members that visit offenders and show support in various ways, help offenders cope with prison life and behavioural patterns change.

'A man who has nothing to lose, is a very dangerous thing,' gives a spin off on totally the opposite behaviour, when he has everything to lose.

Burl Cain adopted the disciplines taught to him in the program called 'How to achieve a close relationship with God'[12] and stated that it was life changing. Though this, he began teaching it to other offenders of all faiths and religions, despite the criticism and sceptical attitude of the community saying, 'It will never work!' He proved them wrong. He teaches exclusively on Christ, but gives the freedom to those being taught to decide for themselves. The certification of the program, stretches as far as training the offender to become a prison minister, prison teacher or prison lawyer.

Today Burl Cain is a prison warden and his revelation statement to the world is: ~'If you educate a criminal, you get an educated criminal but when you morally rehabilitate a criminal, you get a changed man.' As part of the program he teaches offenders to work hard toward cultivating neighbourly love, with the principles of visit your neighbours, talk to each other, console each other and be concerned about each other's well-being. Keep your community and city free from drugs, violence and illegal activity. Do not steal from your neighbour and go to church together. Do not

---

[12] Program written by New Orleans Baptist Theological Seminary: How to achieve a close relationship with God.

use profanity, because once you start using profanity, violence is surely to follow.

Burl Cain believes that unless there is a true conversion deep inside of himself, touching the offender's soul, where no man can fool himself and only God can meet him and he genuinely seeks change and lets go of his anger and finds forgives, he will remain a soulless predator and reject anything the world offers, with his embittered human fragments. Unless he makes peace with God, he will never be rehabilitated.

There are four reasons prisons promote education, to keep prisoners busy, to improve their quality of life, to control their behavioural patterns and to allow them to achieve something useful in their futures. The church must be aware of factors that influence the outcomes of the programs, as negative influence can have the opposite effect and increase recidivism.

Chapter 3   SPIRITUAL DEVELOPMENT

3.1 Defining spiritual growth, spiritual formation and spiritual transformation, in personal maturity and character.

a. Spiritual Growth:

For spiritual growth to take place certain support structures must be put in place, namely prayer partners or intercessors, mentoring or coaching, care or bible study groups.

God calls you by grace, but in order to live out your calling, a growth process needs to take place, which never ends as we continually grow spiritually. Spiritual growth is much like physical growth, from a baby drinking milk to adulthood maturity. Different people have different spiritual needs and different gifts and talents, depending on their calling. Spiritual growth takes place through the power, leading and gifts of the Holy Spirit. Spiritual growth also takes place through prayer, reading God's word, spending quality time with him, fellowship with other Christians, ministry service and evangelism witnessing.

Spiritual growth helps establishing your identity in Christ and to be a better Christian, so your life can count for serving and glorifying God.

There are five factors that cause hindrances to your personal relationship with God, stunting your spiritual growth, namely:

- Being too busy, busy doing the things of God but not busy with God
- Boredom, when your excitement for God is lacking
- Stagnation, when you are trying to overcome weaknesses in your own strength
- The past, when you used to study the bible earnestly and prayed regularly and had a close relationship with God, but lost that loving connection
- Professionalism, your flesh does not want you to serve God

The last command Jesus gave before he left in Matthew 28: 19-20 is 'The Great Commission.' Jesus trained his disciples and left us the precious Holy Spirit, to continue the ministry.

b. Spiritual Formation:

Spiritual formation centres on spiritual birth, conversion, sanctification, circumcision, restoring broken relationships, God's plan for your life, your calling, and the infilling and baptism of the Holy Spirit. It involves the physical body, as that is where we live from, where we seek a more Christ-like life and someone to guide the process, resulting in a relationship of maturity of God.

Spiritual birth is as real as a physical birth, where you accept Jesus Christ as Saviour, as when we are born again we experience many changes, behavioural patterns and characteristics, affecting our conduct (sin or obedience), thought patterns, wills, friends and in displaying acts of obedience. Faith is not a voluntary action of faith, but rather represents an intellectual act of state.

Character always compensates evil with good and leaves judgement in God's hands. Good character refuses to surround itself with evil. Our conversion should be evident to those who know us, pretending to be changed is sinful, with consideration that God sees the heart, not what is reflected outwardly.

Conversion and your calling are inseparable, when you are saved, you are called. God calls us according to his perfect plan for us and this requires dedication and obedience. Your heart needs to be completely yielded to him and doing his will, must always be our ultimate aim.

The best gift God ever gave you was the gift of the Holy Spirit.

The types of questions to ask Christians regarding spiritual formation are the following:

- What is the proper method of prayer, praying directly to God, or do we go through Jesus?
- Is meditation part of Christian faith?
- How do we react when we feel our prayers are hitting the ceiling, not being answered?
- Is living together acceptable? Why/why not?
- Is gambling harmless or acceptable? Why/why not?
- Is masturbation a sin? Why/why not?
- Is it acceptable to enjoy wine or drink alcohol? Why/why not?
- Is body piercing or tattooing acceptable? Why/why not?
- If a Christian commits suicide, will they go to heaven?
- Will a Christian go to hell for smoking, drug abuse?
- If God is loving, why does he not prevent sin?
- Should I allow prison to change me, or should I be part of the change I want to see in prison?

Based on the above questions, Christian education is imperative to spiritual formation, growth and transformation.

c. Spiritual Transformation:

Spiritual transformation causes people to look at their lives differently, to question belief systems and rules they grew up under.

Through spiritual transformation, emotional healing takes place, such as overcoming rejection letting go of past pain, deliverance, distinguishing between heart versus head thought patterns, letting go of anger, forgiveness and putting on the mind of Christ.

Emotional healing in adulthood is imperative if emotional development in childhood was lacking, as not all families are law abiding citizens or have Christian fathers that lead the family as God requires. Some children experienced abuse, early exposure to sex, fatherlessness, parents who were Satanists, drug addicts, or alcoholics, hunger, fending for themselves, foster homes, cruel step-parents, having no love or healthy parent-child cuddling.

God wants to use you, but needs to heal you emotionally first. An egg hardens and a potato softens when boiled. The same sun that hardens clay, melts butter. God loves you too much to leave you as you are, thus transforms you and conforms you, to look more like him.

(*Romans 10:14*) 'How will they hear, if no-one tells them?' May we respectfully add or rephrase for purposes of this book: 'How will they teach, if they are not taught what to say, through sound, bible based Christian education?'

Chapter 4   BRIDGING THE GAP

4.1 Relationships between offenders, victims of crime, the family members of offenders, the community, the church and various Government Departments.

Relationship between offenders and Government Departments

Bridging the gap means that the responsibility for all prisoners is shared between the Correctional Services, Justice, Health and Education Departments, and in the case of children prisoners the Department of Welfare, until their time of sentencing.

Relationship between offenders and victims of crime

The relationship between victim and offender includes true and full confession, forgiveness, examining charge reduction, safety and security and level of exposure. The level of trust in this relationship is based on the aggressiveness of the crime committed and future harm or victimisation that could be caused, vulnerability of the victim and offender as well as investigative guidelines.

An example of this would be an offender that murdered someone by accident while under the influence of drugs or alcohol, asking the victim forgiveness and the victim agrees to forgive. Another example would be a serial stalker who the victim knows if he is released from prison, he will stalk her again, so even though the victim forgives, they are weary and vulnerable and would most likely move to a new town and not have any contact once the offender is released from prison. A third example would be a paedophile who killed someone's daughter and the parents refuse to forgive, holding on to a grudge and promising the offender that if they ever got released, there would be 'mob justice' from the community or the father of the child himself will kill the perpetrator. Thus, it is not always only the victim that is vulnerable or susceptible to receiving harm, but the offender too. A fourth example is a drug user that never paid the drug lord and once released the drug lord's gang will descend on him.

Trust is earned and an offender would have to work very hard to prove he has changed and to build on any relationship with the victims and their families. Angry family members could be set out for revenge with years of resentment built up over time, with fantasies of hurting the offender relived over and over again. Victims who were violently raped, then fell pregnant or contracted HIV/Aids, have been deeply hurt with reminders daily staring them in the face, find it very difficult to forgive, not realising or grasping the concept that forgiveness sets them free.

Mediation is imperative in these situations. Not everyone is willing to forgive and not everyone is willing to tell the truth at the Truth and Reconciliation Commission.

What is Stockholm Syndrome (SS)?

Stockholm Syndrome (SS) is a psychological response which occurs when abuse victims bond with their abusers, or hostages bond, pledge or connection with their captors which takes place over a few days, months or even years of the abuse or captivity. (SS) people often develop post-traumatic stress, nightmares, insomnia, flashbacks, confusion and are easily startled and have difficulty trusting others.

With this syndrome, victims tend to sympathise with their abusers, which is often the opposite of fear, terror, contempt, anxiety and uncertainty. Over time, some victims develop positive feelings towards their abusers or captors, often helping them escape if the police are on their tail. The victim being brainwashed and lied to by the captor or abuser, may even develop negative feelings towards the police. This does not occur with every victim and is a condition that psychologists or doctors describe as a coping mechanism which helps the victim cope with the trauma or terrifying situation. Due to threats or lies, they avoid retaliation.

Victims realise that as much as they hate the abuser, they need the abuser for survival. The abusers often go to great lengths to convince the victims that only the abuser loves or cares about them, their families have forgotten them or written them off, or believe them to be dead.

In the case of child brides, the abusers make the victim believe the marriage and under-age sex, is God's will, so the victim submits under their authority, but remains emotionally broken and unhappy. The victim may even begin to see the 'good' in their captives or abusers and want to help them, instead of run away from them. Ultimately (SS) is loyalty and attachment to abusers, based in fear.

(SS) may occur in different situations, but the focus for this book is on pedophilia

- Cults or Sects with abusive and controlling leaders
- Pedophilia
- Child abuse
- Sex trafficking trade
- Sports coaching
- Boss and employee
- Parents and children abuse
- Abductions or kidnappings
- Incest
- Bullying
- Marital rape
- Drug lord, drug addict
- Pimp, prostitute
- Abusers, either husbands or wives
- Adoptees, placed in abusive families

Relationship between offenders and the church

For the purposes of this book, I asked six Pastors if they would welcome ex-offenders into their churches. I received very interesting responses. Three replied no, as it would either unnerve or intimidate the congregation or the pastor would have to first find out if the ex-offender has a 'selfish reason' for wanting to be in church (seeking employment, networking, hoping for monetary handouts from congregation members). Two replied yes, the one Pastor said everyone deserves a second chance, the other Pastor said that as long as the ex-offenders do not all sit together because they will try to form a community of their own, while he wants his church to fellowship and mix with everyone. One said maybe, depending on the crimes they committed.

(Osmer: 2008) The church should ensure that bible based prison programs that encourage and support offenders in a manner of spiritual and moral transformation, that begins while they are in prison and continues after they are released. In his study he determined that there are not enough skilled persons such as social workers, spiritual workers, counsellors and ministers to volunteer pro bono for offenders and due to understaffing not enough prison staff to run programs. The church needs to step up and take responsibility for effective religious rehabilitation, to contribute towards reducing recidivism.

For full effectiveness the church needs to evaluate which Christian educational programs are being rendered and prayerfully consider which are much needed and consider delivering sound doctrinal missional and theological teachings that stop false teachings by others rendering services without any training.

Relationship between offenders and their family members

Offenders are not easily welcomed back into communities or families, unless drastic change is evident, but particularly if they are known to be sex offenders. Most family members, usually with the exception of the mother of the offender, do not want the offender to come back home after release from prison, unless they see evidence of drastic change. They remain unconvinced that the offender has experienced transformation. During a Restorative Justice session run through Hope prison Ministry, an offender apologized to his family for the hurt he caused and said this time, he promises to be different. The family, in tears shook their heads and asked what is so different about this time? He had disappointed them and hurt them so many times in the past. He answered, 'This time, I have Jesus in my heart!'

Another occasion, during a Restorative Justice program, a young girl in prison was sobbing with tears over her paedophile father that sexually abused her since age 8, with her mother's full knowledge of what was happening through the years, the girl was now 19 years old. Her father sexually abused her to the point that she fell pregnant with his baby at age 11 and gave birth to a little girl at age 12. She hated the baby, because every time she looked at her, the baby reminded her of her father. Her father lied to the rest of the family and the community and the school, to say his daughter was promiscuous and the father of the baby unknown. The young girl killed the baby and while in prison, her father died in a horrendous car accident. The last words she ever spoke to her father ring in her ears like a church bell daily, 'I hate you. May you burn in hell one day!' Through the Restorative Justice program, she learned to forgive her father, although he has already died. Her mother, who made no attempt to stop the abuse, was also forgiven but not until after she made no secret of telling her mother exactly how she felt all those years, afraid, vulnerable and neglected. She found peace after the program, although she never wanted to see her mother ever again.

Some offenders are perpetrators, but some are victims too. Most offenders are attached to their mothers, even hardened criminals and gangsters soften when you talk about their mother.

Going back to the family after release, often means living in a Wendy House, a small wooden structure attached to a home, or standing in a back yard, with many other people already living inside it. Poor family networks, absence of role models and parental guidance and support, lack of counselling, unemployment and poverty, makes it difficult to adjust as the family often sees the ex-offender as *'just another mouth to feed.'*

Family members feel that Christian educational programs should be run in community halls for all youth. Programs run in prisons should be sustained after the offender's release, and should include support groups for their family members, since the family members play a pivotal role in the ex-offender's rehabilitation and reintegration.

Relationship between offenders and community members

Offenders feel that community members are not very forgiving, but rather judgmental and skeptical. A *'keep your door locked, because that monster is out of prison!'* approach is adopted by community members.

If a mother and child is loved and respected by their community and a pedophile-necrophile kills the child and sexually abuses the corpse, in some communities society members will fight for that mother.

Unless controlled by the police, they will take matters into their own hands and burn the perpetrator's house, scorn the perpetrator's family members, or similar.

There are usually monthly community meetings held with community leaders, local police officers and parole officers there will be announced those who are being let out of prison on parole, to bring awareness and warning. If the community has had communication from the prison officials and are convinced that the offender has attended programs that promote change and they feel safe, they will welcome the ex-offender and mentor them, pray for them and encourage them – however, they will keep an eagle eye on them and monitor their progress and behaviour patterns.

Victims of violent or sexual crimes

Violent crimes cause the victims to feel a sense of uncertainty, insecurity, disempowerment and vulnerability, leading to high levels of stress for their personal safety. Violent victimisation can also be linked to fear, depression, anxiety, confusion, depression, anger, nightmares, night sweats, and sadness, which in turn causes illnesses such as Post Traumatic Stress Disorder (PTSD) or mental problems. This cycle of emotions, then turns into a pool of different negative responses such as self-blame, shame, worry, reduced self-worth, inadequacy to protect the family and embarrassment and/or destructive behaviour which may even result in suicide.

Many are left with physical impairments after violent crimes, such as ending in in wheelchairs, loss of a limb, heart problems, aches and pains in their bodies, headaches, loss of an eye etc. Loss of sleep and the taking of anti-depressants or sleeping tablets or other sedatives brings deterioration as their quality of life starts to decrease which then filters out to affecting their employment, recreation, social interaction and family life.

To avoid violent crimes, people start to relocate to other areas where they feel safer, which also adversely affects local businesses in the area as most who can afford to, move away.

4.2 Sex offender registry.

The National Register of Sexual Offenders (NRSO) was put in place to stop the frequency of serious incidents against children and mentally disabled people, by placing on the register all the details of convicted sexual offenders. Through this register, employees, community and family members, police, welfare, social development department, justice department and correctional services, have certain obligations and structure to put in place to protect children, from these perpetrators.

The Criminal Law Amendment Act, 2007[13] *covers five offences, namely:*

---

[13] Act 32, of 2007 www.justice.gov.org

- Sexual grooming
- Flashing
- Exposure to pornography
- Causing children to witness sexual assault
- Creation of child pornography

With sex crimes on the increase, in particular crimes committed by paedophiles, how effective is the register? Especially since the general public has no access to it, it remains confidential, unless an employer such as crèches, hospitals, schools, ministries involving children, or the police department does a police clearance screening on the individual in question. Notwithstanding, the sex offender may not open his/her own business involving contact with children and any employer discovering that they have in their employ a sex offender, would need to apply stringent measures to ensure the employee, aka sex offender is working in a child-free zone. The employer however, cannot monitor the employee after hours, for violation of their privacy.

One good point remains, that any sex-offender that has served his sentence and parole, after a five or ten year period[14] may get their name removed from the register, through a letter written to the Department of

---

[14] 10 year period lapses after the date of the conviction for that offence, barring they have not reoffended. Before submitting an application for expungement of a conviction, a clearance certificate showing 10 years has elapsed after the conviction/s and sentence/s, must be obtained from the Criminal Record Centre of the SAPS.

Social Development,[15] but will still have the information reflect on the police clearance certificate that they were a sex offender and their name has been removed, giving the person an opportunity to make an informed decision to employ them or use them for ministry, or not.

If the NSRO was made available to all members of the public, it could cause violent, mass mob actions and reactions, expressly if the perpetrator offended against children, This scenario gives the sexual offender an advantageous edge, to 'hide the crime' and make a new start. The community where the offender would be living, would be at a possible disadvantage, not knowing the offender has such a record.

In an interview conducted between the Captain of the South African Police Services (SAPS) in Atlantis and Pastor Jerome Samuels, it was stated by the Captain, 'Sometimes people are released without (SAPS) knowledge.' (SAPS) is expected to protect the community, but the lack of communication between the Department of Correctional Services (DCS) and (SAPS) is sorely lacking and poses a problem.

---

[15] The NRSO contains names of offenders against children and mentally disabled people, while the Department of Social Development Register, lists offenders of all forms of child abuse.

Early release parole conditions

Recent changes to the 'South African Prison Legislation' states that prisoners who have served their sentences, due to overcrowding in prisons, may be released earlier, based on one of the following conditions:

- Correctional supervision outside of prison
- Reside at a half way rehabilitation centre
- Community service
- House arrest
- Ongoing treatment program
- Pay compensation money to the victim
- Employment
- <u>MUST</u> have a home address
- Paedophiles may not hang around places within a radius of 6 Kilometres of a school or crèche, nor work at any company that has anything to do with children or mentally disabled persons.

Through these parole conditions, the Department of Correctional Services claim a 90% success rate of early release.

Ex-offenders however claim the employment system is exploited, as prisons help them find employment on farms, while prison staff are given gifts for their efforts by the farmers. The first thing that goes wrong during his employ, or if the farmer mistreats the ex-offender, the ex-offender is automatically accused and slammed back into prison, accused of breaking his parole conditions. The labour rates paid to ex-offenders on the farms are between R2.00 and R2.50 a day.[16] The fortunate ones picking olives they would receive R0.40c per kilogram, picking only 3 crates a day of 25kg each, earns them R30.00 a day.

[16] H.J. Bruyn 'An overview of the treatment of offenders in prison and correctional supervision' (Pretoria Human Science Research Council, 1992) article Lorraine Glanz (Editor) managing Crime in the New South Africa.

Chapter 5   EDUCATIONAL SYSTEMS AND METHODOLOGY

5.1 The inmate's rights to education, according to Government legislation.

'We are polarized as a nation, on the question of how to deal with crime and how to treat prisoners. Perhaps we are much less polarized on the question of whether it is in our self-interest to make sure our ex-prisoners are literate. This is the question we raise by issuing this report: Should these captives also be students?'[17]

The equality clause of the South African Constitution outlaws all discrimination based on religion, conscience, culture and belief, the statement rings loud and clear, 'South Africa belongs to all who live in it, united in our diversity.' The constitution also gives the right to 'freedom of religion, belief and opinion,' (Section 15)[18]. Discrimination based on religion or culture is prohibited. The constitution tells us that this kind of observance must be conducted under the following conditions:

- In accordance with the rules of 'appropriate public authorities'
- On an 'equitable basis'

---

[17] Excerpt from Up and Locked Out pdf, Barton and Coley, 1996, Page 31.
[18] Basic Education Rights Handbook, Chapter Ten, Page 188-189, Religion and culture in public education in South Africa.

- In a manner that ensures that attendance is 'free and voluntary'

Religion is ordinarily concerned with personal faith and belief, while culture generally relates to traditions and beliefs developed through the years by ancestors, but the two normally overlap and the constitution protects discrimination that flows from interference with the two practices. Freedom of religion, like other human rights, is to be respected, promoted and protected by the relevant and trusted authorities to comply with the applicable laws, for the prison environment.[19] Although religion could represent Islam, Satanism, Rastafarian, Christianity, Judaism, New Age, Hinduism or other belief systems, it is a right afforded to the prisoner, to practice whatever faith he/she chooses. These principles make provision for international human rights and are classified by many scholars as sources of international law.[20]

In terms of the constitution obligations, includes the prisoner's right to reading materials and every prison institution shall have a library. The library is to be sufficiently stocked with recreational and instructional books.[21] The Standard Minimum Rules (SMR) provides for the right to further education for all prisoners and compulsory basic education for illiterates and juvenile prisoners. The education prisoners receive is integrated

---

[19] White Paper on Corrections in South Africa (2005), Journal on the study of religion, Page 1 (2019).
[20] Mansell & Open Shaw 2013:17, Aust 2010:5, Dugard 2005:27.
[21] s35(2)(e) of paragraph 40, Standard Minimum Rules (SMR).

into the educational system of the country, thus when they are released, they are able to continue their education.

The Department of Correctional Services (DCS) provides education and training development skills in order to rehabilitate prisoners and to contribute towards affecting behavioural changes. The prisons are given opportunities to work with Spiritual Care Workers, Psychologists, Educationists, Social Workers and Religious Workers. The programs the prisoners participate in, are provided in partnership with NGO's, NPO's, churches and tertiary institutions and equip prisoners with skills, values and knowledge.

The (DCS) budget, caters mostly for prisoners affected by HIV/AIDS, due to the high incidences among them,[22] than for any other program. Due to overcrowding in the prisons, budgeting for nutrition (food for prisoners) takes prevalence over education. ABET also forms part of the education options, provided by the (DCS) for a balanced and integrated approach. If prisoners wish to study Christian educational programs, they have to apply to institutions outside of (DCS) for sponsorships or bursaries. Lacking in the budget, is adequate allocation for Early Childhood Development (ECD) for children born in prisons, through incarcerated mothers.

---

[22] Overcrowding from increase in prison population, constitutes more prison rapes and with that, the risks and rates of HIV/Aids rises higher.

It is a well-known fact that prisons are closed and secured environment, creating fertile ground for prison authorities to violate the Christian educational rights of prisoners. The UN have legal obligations related to the human rights and protection of prisoners and the standard minimum rules for the treatment of prisoners was initially adopted by the General Assembly in 1955 and revised in 2015. The Nelson Mandela Rules are not as binding in nature, however are universally acknowledged as a minimum standard for the detention of prisoners, have significant value and influence. These are indirect obligations.

(Anon: 1995) The Nelson Mandela Rules on the prevention of crime and the treatment of offenders, which was adopted by the United Nations Congress, held in Geneva in 1955. They were set apart to protect human rights and to give guidance to prison authorities how to guard offenders on a daily basis. Section 41 and 42 of the Rules focuses on authorities allowing religion as part of the offender's daily routine, also allowing religious organisations access to hold regular services to assist offenders with their spiritual needs and the relevant church or FBO must provide the proper tools to assist with the offender's rehabilitation.

We determine that South Africa is a functional, democratic society that is based on human dignity, equality and freedom. The right of prisoners to freedom of religion extends further than organizing gatherings and training of chaplains.

It goes against the preceding backdrop that prisoner's rights to freedom of religion, cannot be separated from the right to human dignity. In practice, many prisoners are still denied access to Christian education, often the spiritual care worker will only grant it as a 'reward' for good behaviour, instead of a tool for a better life. Prison authorities should ensure freedom of religion is practiced, respected and consistent.

Solitary confinement and education

Solitary confinement is a forbidding and humiliating punishment, which allows for no human contact. Solitary confinement makes it difficult to tell one day from a thousand others. Solitary confinement is a prison within a prison, it is like being buried alive. It is a sad thing to watch a man go insane, because he cannot handle the pressure, the claustrophobia of the tiny box and it is even sadder when you see the man's spirit traumatised, from the depth his soul. Solitary gives lone offenders an opportunity to talk through walls for years and never get to see the face of who you are talking to and allows a man to be continually surrounded by misery. Privileges, including food, visitors and education are either removed, restricted and prohibited. In the 1900's this punishment was accompanied by whippings and additional labour. This inhumanity is known as one of the cruellest punishments on God's earth: A slow, merciless and silent killer.

(White Paper Corrections: 2005) brought new developments and held more promise for better conditions with the emphasis on rehabilitation, instead of punishment, with three fundamental viewpoints of retribution as the delivery of punishment, utilitarian as the criminal justice system bringing about beneficial change in reducing recidivism and humanitarian as deciding on what form and length of punishment, is appropriate for the crime committed. Two other behavioural sciences were later added, the rehabilitation model and the restitution view. Ultimately, the retributivists wanted offenders to get their just desserts, the utilitarian's wanted to deter them from offending again and the rehabilitationers wanted to cure them, yet none had much to say about the victims of the offences committed, who suffered the most.

Taking education away as a 'privilege benefit,' as opposed to what it really is, a 'basic human right' is not effective. Solitary confinement prisoners sit and stare a four walls for 23 hours a day, with very little stimuli, which does not aid rehabilitation.

5.2 Diverse Christian educational programs taught and not taught in prisons.

Christian prison ministry organisations offer programs that are bible based, fun and lower level educational, however findings show that Christian education impacts offenders in that they are amenable to training and education.[23] These can generally improve their behavioural patterns, based on their perception of the teacher's real concern, personal interest and dynamic instruction. A few researches interestingly found no evidence that adult Christian education had any positive effects on recidivism, however that inmates exposed to Christian educational programs, have lower recidivism rates than non-participants.[24]

Offering programs is a mechanism prisons use to rehabilitate and reintegrate. The programs are defined within the guidelines of the Department of Correctional Service's booklet called 'Correctional Programs Targeting Offending Behaviour, which includes 8 specific programs, facilitated by Correctional Intervention Officials (CIO's):

- Anger Management, raising awareness of causes and symptoms of anger and how to manage it.
- Crossroads, corrects basic behaviour patterns.
- Preparatory Program on Sexual Offences, addressing sexually offending behaviour, through applicable knowledge and skills.
- Pre-Release Program, prepares offender for successful reintegration by assisting them with coping mechanism skills.

---

[23] D. Lipton, R. Martinson and J. Wilks, The Effectiveness of Correctional Treatment, Published Praeger, New York, 1975.
[24] R. Luiden and D. Perry, An Evaluation of Prison Education Programs, Canadian journal of criminology, 1984.

- Substance Abuse Correctional Program, assists offenders gain insight on the negative effects and ripple effects of substance abuse of all kinds.
- Restorative Justice Program, prepares offenders for reintegration, mediation between victim and offender and offender family members.
- Behaviour Modification Program, raises awareness of gang related activities and their negative consequences, assists the offender to cope in prison without gang affiliation.
- New Beginnings Orientation Program, trains the offender to be aware of their surroundings and assists with adjustments into the prison system.

The Sexual Offence's Program does not include any diversion programs, or inserts that are tailored to assist pedophiles or necrophiles.

Prison ministries offer a wide scope of Christian based rehabilitation programs that are extensively used throughout the world. Prison ministry leaders are to go through a screening process prior to teaching in prisons, which includes a police clearance certificate. This way, paedophiles will not be allowed to teach children or juveniles.

Distance learning for offenders, is as important as attending classes. (Gaes: 2008) findings reached a conclusion that although methodology limitations associated with examined research, distance learning prisoner education programs on recidivism reduction made a positive impact, these sentiments were echoed by (Gerber and Fritsch: 1995) and (Jensen and Reed: 2006).[25]

Some famous programs in South Africa include Restorative Justice (Victims and perpetrator healing), Fatherhood (majority of prisoners come from fatherless homes), Crossroads (choices), Kairos International (healing through mentoring), Prison Fellowship International (behavioural intervention) Nehemiah Bible Institute (church leadership and ministry development, pastoral counselling and prison correspondence courses based on life skills, recidivism, leaving gangs, forgiveness)[26], CABSA (HIV and Aids awareness and prevention), Networking for Christ SA (pre and post release offender, victims of crime, families of criminals, assist ex-offenders with job readiness, reintegration, gender based violence and victim empowerment)[27] and Heartlines (emotional healing).

---

[25] Education in Prisons: Studying through Distance Learning, book by Emma Hughes (Published by Ashgate, California, USA) © 2012, Page 149.

[26] Mrs Mercial Adonis, contact interview, testifies to the impact their 29 different programs make, the prisons welcome these programs, used in 96% of prisons in South Africa, and Texas USA.

[27] Managing Director Mr Ulrich Lottering, Contact interview, has sound records of reduced recidivism and behavioural changes, his programs bridge the gap between offender, family and victims of crime.

Other non- Christian educational programs include NICRO (National Institute for Crime Prevention and the Reintegration of Offenders, arts and culture, agriculture and psychology) as well as Prison Yoga Project (non-Christian yoga), Muslim Council (Islamic teachings of the Koran), Mindfulness Meditation (Buddhist teachings), Mormons (Latter-day saints), Satanism (Devil worship), Rastafarians (Rasta), Catholic Priests (Catholicism) and more. At present, a group of Satanists are fighting in the High Court in Queensland Australia, to legalize Satanism being taught in all government schools, so it could be assumed that it would just be a matter of time, before they insist on it being taught in prisons.

The selection of which prisoners attend which programs is often random, based on good behaviour in the cell, as opposed to which religion the offender actually belongs to. Thus, Muslims are regularly roped into Christian classes, Rasta's into Muslim classes and Christians into Mindfulness classes (as examples) which poses a problem. The offender will not object, as it means free time out of their cell, if they are men they may perhaps meet nice girls that are prison ministry leaders, perhaps receive great food as part of the program, or perhaps be able to manipulate someone into buying them much needed phone cards, stamps, envelopes, money, or other needs. If a Christian educator teaches offenders that meditation is necessary, spending quality time with God and meditating on his word, they will easily identify with yoga or mindfulness which is nothing to do with Christianity, but may well think it a correct manner of worship, if they meditate on biblical scripture while doing yoga or mindfulness, while it operates under the Kundalini spirit and brings dangerous spiritual curses, over the Christian's life.

A challenge in presenting Christian education in prisons remains the fact that there are many different denominations represented through prison ministry leaders, pastors and teachers with different statements of faith, cultural backgrounds and belief systems that are given access by the prison chaplains, to minister to and educate inmates. These diverse systems frequently cause confusion and oppression, rather than liberation for the inmates, through the varied pluralistic knowledge and sentiments that they obtain. While Yoga would raise eyebrows among Christians, non-Christians would relish the relaxation techniques.

Satanism is legal and allows gangsters, who feel they have nothing to lose, the legal right to commit heinous crimes. Although many gangsters may not be outright Satanists, they operate under Satan's vices, in rank, authority and intimidation. The most notorious gangs in the South African prisons, are the **26's, 27's and the 28's**. Satan comes to kill, steal and destroy (*John 10:10-29*).

- The 26's stand for money (steal).
- The 27's stand for murder (kill).

- The 28's stand for sex (destroy).[28]

Encompassing on Christian educational programs and activities offered in South Africa:

Fatherhood program:	The majority of prisoners come from fatherless homes, mothers working two jobs to support the family, children left to their own devices through no fault of their own, boredom and lack of mentorship break the cycle of knowing their identity, program promotes God as perfect Father.
Crossroads	Based on making good choices.
Kairos International	Healing through six months of mentoring,

[28] South African Prison Ministry Leadership Workshop Training Manual, Published by CLF 2019, Author Val Hamann

	weekend program of the making of six prominent masks, motivational talks, group discussions, fun activities, a very moving forgiveness ceremony, foot washing ceremony and sound bible based teachings.
Prison Fellowship International	Behavioural intervention, between six and twenty-four months of mentoring, post release support up to 12 months, inner change and freedom, training and support to Wardens.
Hope Prison Ministry	Restorative Justice, promotes victims, perpetrator and

family mediation and healing.

Nehemiah Bible Institute

Church leadership and ministry development, pastoral care counselling and prison correspondence courses based on life skills, recidivism, leaving gangs, spiritual growth and forgiveness, annual Christmas card drive to help inmates stay in touch with their families, annual art competition to develop their artistic skills.[29]

Bible Media:

The correspondence programs they offer include:

---

[29]Mrs Mercial Adonis, contact interview, testifies to the impact their 29 different programs make, the prisons welcome these programs, used in 96% of prisons in South Africa, and Texas USA.

	Liberty in Captivity, The Only way Out, Socially Speaking, Your Life: Your Choice, My Pledge: Committed to Change and Masquerade: what mask are you hiding behind?
Team Impact University America	Ministry certificates and degrees via correspondence studies.
CABSA	HIV and Aids awareness and prevention classes and correspondence courses, family support.
Networking for Christ SA	Pre and post release support to

	offenders, victims of crime and families of criminals. Assist ex-offenders with job readiness and reintegration. Gender based violence and victim empowerment, anger and forgiveness courses, overcoming rejection and embracing self-esteem.[30]
Heartlines	Emotional healing from past trauma.
Heart Sparks CLF Publishers	Women's prison ministry program, dealing with past trauma such as divorce, death, loss, forgiveness

---

[30] Managing Director Mr Ulrich Lottering, Contact interview, has sound records of reduced recidivism and behavioural changes, his programs bridge the gap between offender, family and victims of crime.

and putting your life back together.

Choir and Bands	Prisons have choirs and bands, musical instruments are donated by outside companies or ministries, choirs compete against other prisons, bands travel to outside prison events such as the annual prison expo. These music based programs are mostly Christian based hymns and songs.

Other non- Christian educational programs and activities include:

NICRO	National Institute for Crime Prevention and the Reintegration of Offenders, with

secular psychology
based principles,
arts and culture,
agriculture

Prison Yoga Project
Yoga therapy, meditation, kundalini spirit
Muslim Council
Islamic teachings of the Koran
Mindfulness Meditation
Buddhist teachings, chanting, meditation
Mormons
Latter-day saints, Mormon teachings
Satanism
Devil worship, setting curses, chanting, blood drinking
Rastafari
Rasta teachings, Rasta hair dregs
Catholic Priests
Catholicism, Idol worship, Rosary
Gumboot Dancing
Traditional African gumboot dancing

Drumming	Rhythm and chanting, stirring up of ancestral spirits
Sports	Soccer, Basketball, Rugby, Netball, Boxing – prisons compete against other prisons

Dog training unit	Offenders are allowed to work with the dog training unit, classes run outside of prison cells, which is therapeutic and promotes teaching responsibility, discipline and love
Clothing manufacturing	Classes for offenders to design and make children's clothing, sewing, patternmaking, beadwork.
Leather work	Teaches offenders to repair shoes and handbags.

5.3 Methodology and impact of Christian educational systems, taught in prisons.

'In some circumstances, a refusal to be defeated, is a refusal to be educated.' ~Quote Margaret Halsey[31]

---

[31] Justice Denied, book by David Klatzow, Page 131.

Christian education programs positively affect behavioural changes, so they are used for that reason by spiritual care workers and prison authorities as a form of controlling the prison population more effectively, benefitting the prison and its system more than the effects and impact benefitting the actual prisoner. Most prisons in USA are privatized, for the benefits of the private companies making money out of cheap labour of the prisoners.

There are 2.3[32] Million prisoners in the USA, part of which only 300 US citizens and 14,000 are foreign nationals are housed in privatized prisons, who get deported after their sentence is 'complete.'

The word complete is a farce, as most prisoners are housed as awaiting trial for years before their sentencing and even after their sentencing, are held back from receiving parole or early release, as the prisons have a Memorandum of Understanding (MOU) with US Government that the privatized prisons need to have a 90% occupancy, in order for the private companies to make profits.

Christian educational programs are thus utilized in these situations to bring 'comfort and hope' to the offenders and change their behavioural patterns, keeping them under condescending control, as

---

[32] https://en.wikipedia.org/wiki/United_States_incarceration_rate - Downloaded May 2021.

opposed to them actually knowing God and finding salvation.

It is essential that faith based programs continue to be evaluated and added to the prison, with the same standards as secular programs. Christian educational programs run in South African prisons, have a need for programs that extend Gender Based Violence in the area of a broader base of sex crimes. Even very few secular programs, deal with pedophilia and necrophilia. Faith based programs are attractive to the prison spiritual care workers and the prisoners, as most South African prisoners are open to Christianity, barring gangsters.

The prisoner, also needs a network of support to help assimilate back into society. For some offenders though, the Christian education only lasts for as long as the prison sentence does. The offender's ability to find a network of support is difficult, especially if his own family environment is not a stable social structure.[33]

Both faith based and secular programs provide critical social environments that determine the success of an offender's rehabilitation, however Christian education is a significant indicator and predictor of reduced recidivism and promotes accountability, following the offender's release from prison. Release is granted when offenders exhibit good behaviour and minimum infractions and violations.

---

[33] Deloitte (2016) Page 26, Framework data and methodology.

The rationale for recidivism also pertains to aftercare services, family support and stability, volunteers, mentors and continuation of attending church, studying and employment. When the ex-offender enters society he/she faces many challenges and having the stigma of a prison record, does not help.

There are various methods that programs are taught in South African prisons:

As a mentor or prison ministry leader you need to be ready for any situation, or change, most of the time in prison, conventional teaching methods are utilized as no laptops, cell phones, plastic bags, or cameras, knives, scissors, glue, or money are allowed inside. Food may be taken in for closing ceremonies at the end of a program, with prior permission of the prison head. During the programs being presented, offenders may confess other crimes they have committed, however the mentor or prison ministry leader must keep the information confidential unless the offender gives the permission to speak out, as a way of 'coming clean' which happens during Christian based programs. All offenders are roll called / counted prior to the program and after the program.

- **Prison library,** offenders attending the program get called to the prison library, some sit on desks, some on old chairs, some on the floor and some on the window sill. The door gets closed, often with no warden inside and the mentor or prison ministry leader stands in front and teaches, with workbooks, paper, pencils. Pencils are counted prior to handing out and counted on return as a sharp pencil could be used as a weapon to stab eyes out, or into ears. It is uncomfortable for them to write with books on their laps.

- **Classrooms with tables and chairs,** maximum thirty six offenders, six per table, with one prison ministry leader per table, prison ministry leader in front of class. Sometimes a black board and chalk is available. Offenders may have workbooks and pencils, which must be handed back at the end of the lesson, as a sharp pencil could be used as a weapon to stab eyes out, or into ears.
- **Ministry preaching class,** inmates sit on benches, listen to the sermon. Holy Communion can take place, but no glass containers may be used, as broken glass can be used as a weapon.
- **Weekend programs,** offenders sit in a large hall with the prison ministry leadership team. No offender may go to the toilet alone, a prison ministry leader must accompany them, wait outside the door and escort them back to their table. Pencils, pens, crayons and glue must be counted prior to offenders entering the room and collected and recounted, prior to them leaving.

- If an item stolen it must be reported. Offenders must be served food and refreshment drinks while they are seated at their tables and not stand in a queue to wait for their food.
- **Art classes,** usually ten offenders at a time, sit in a circle and the art teacher provides all the art supplies and sketch books. Stationary must be counted prior to offenders entering the room and collected and recounted, prior to them leaving.
- **Outside classes or events,** a tent is erected outside the prison cells, but inside the prison grounds, with large speakers, a PA system, a band, chairs for the guests, offenders usually sit on the grass.
- **Dog training classes,** held near the kennels at the dog unit, but only a few prisons have this privilege of teaching offenders to train the dogs in detecting drugs and further illegal substances, as well as pin down and control offenders when gang fights break out.

Prison pedagogy:

Pedagogy explained: The applied method and practise of teaching experience, as an academic subject or theoretical concept, in a relationship where teacher and offender produce work and learn together; learn from and teach each other; discover different and common points of view and a dialectical relationship between the outward material world and the inner spiritual world.

It tracks the mirror images of the 'pedagogy of the oppressed inside prison' and the 'pedagogy of liberty outside of prison.'

Pedagogy has different approaches and attributes:

- Constructive
- Integrative
- Interactive
- Collaborative
- Reflective
- Inquiry Based
- Innovative
- Creative

Fear, shame and exposure are three challenges for offenders that attend Christian education classes. Fear manifests in various manners, from violence to silence. An environment governed by fear, is always tense and testing. Shame and guilt can be misconstrued in prisons. Guilt says, 'I have done something bad.' Shame has an ethical response, 'I am bad because of what I have done.' A feeling of hopelessness, is a form of silence. Joining a gang, is indirectly an act of violence. By removing fear, guilt and shame, the offender's identity of being made in the image of God is established.

To overcome these challenges, there are some elements that need to be embraced by Christian education, which includes allowing offenders to have their voices amplified, to tell of their own experience, without being ridiculed, victimised or blamed.

Faith based educational programs in prisons seem to lack the depth that higher education offers. While promoting God awareness and redemptive biblical knowledge, Christian education deprives the prisoner of political, financial, mathematical, medical, scientific, skills development, employment readiness and life skills knowledge. Yet, many testify to the positive influence and behavioural changes that take place, of those offenders attending Christian educational programs, notwithstanding the cost effectiveness of presenting these programs, through volunteers and community involvement.

The programs vary according to structure, duration, materials and effectiveness. More efficient methodology needs to be applied in order to more accurately evaluate the impact of faith based programs.

The point of exodus for learning support in the inclusive education in South Africa, is the pedagogy of possibility that takes into consideration barriers of learning, different learning styles and different levels of intelligence (Department of Education: 2002).

To achieve these benefits, there are three categories of education that need to be taught in prisons:

General	Subjects such as science, maths, religion, geography, history, languages, philosophy, health, social science, etc.
Vocational	Education which aims to equip people with knowledge, know-how skills and competencies.
Non-formal	Focuses on assisting offenders with issues such as anger and forgiveness, overcoming rejection and embracing self-esteem, critical thinking skills, reintegration coping mechanisms, technology, workplace skills, etc.

According to (Dammer: 2002), reasons for Christian education for offenders are:

- Many gain direction and meaning for life, as God will direct their steps.
- Offenders prefer to submit to God's will, not their own and often come to accept that were they not in prison, they would never have known God, or accepted Jesus Christ, or they could have been more deeply involved in crime or gangsterism, or be dead.
- Christian education gives offenders 'peace of mind' and leads them to a level of personal contentment, especially those who have long or life sentences.

- Improves the offender's self-confidence and their self-concept, assisting them to let go of guilt and pain, accept that they came from dysfunctional homes, have remorse for their crimes, etc.
- Promotes emotional and psychological benefits, as offenders learn self-control which assists with them obeying prison rules and regulations.

On a negative note, Christian education classes presents them with an opportunity to conduct the following behaviour:

- Hold a prison ministry leader hostage, to riot in the prisons, to have demands met.
- Smuggle contraband, including drugs, cigarettes, or weapons and inside information.
- Seek vulnerable prison ministry leaders to manipulate, or start a relationship with for benefits of material goods, legal assistance, visitations, musical instruments, radios and/or money.
- Only seek to enjoy the food prison ministry leaders bring to the classes.
- Social interaction with other offenders.
- Pathways to communication for gang members to carry messages and threats.

(Murphy and Souto-Otero: 2013) show in their research that education is one key aspect of the rehabilitative process, which an offender can engage in while in prison. For the prison, it means keeping the prisoner busy, helping them make good use of their sentence time, to change their attitude and behavioural patterns and improve their chances of being employed. To the prisoner means the difference between success and failure after release. There is however, still the reality that not every prisoner that is granted education, secular or Christian, will understand the reasons or consequences, or take responsibility for the crimes they committed. The motivation of the offender enrolling on any these programs, must also be determined prior to them attending.

I spoke to three offenders during writing this book[34], to ask about the impact or non-impact that Christian programs have on their spiritual growth, *participant one* indicated that due to not ever attending them in the past, he believes is why he kept coming back to prison and attending the programs now have helped him cope with his wife that left him, to forgive her and still try to maintain his relationship with his children. He believes that diversion programs should be run in schools to warn youngsters and save them from coming to this horrible place, prison. *Participant two* indicated that although he attends Christian programs, he is still not ready to leave the 'number'/gang. Sadly, he stated further that he is going to need the gangs for when he

---

[34] For the safety and security protocols of offenders, their names cannot be mentioned.

gets out, because nobody else will support him. *Participant three* indicated that he has learned how to administer self-control, let go of his anger, forgive his father for being absent, love those around him and handle difficult problems differently, instead of handling all situations with inner anger and violence. He also further stated that no longer cries at night when no-one sees his tears, but sleeps peacefully knowing God and his angels are watching over him. He cannot wait to get out, to support his mother and sisters.

'Any programs run inside prison, are only effective, if what the prisoner learned, is applied to their practical, everyday lives.' ~Quote, Pastor Jerome September.

Faith based programs are effective in that they promote the statement of assistance to the offender as 'I can do it, through God's strength...' where secular programs promote the statement 'I can do, it through my own strength...'

A prison sentence is not enough on its own, to rehabilitate offenders. For offenders, having a God who 'cares about them and loves them unconditionally,' when in reality their own friends and family members 'have given up on them,' brings comfort, calm and acceptance. Kingdom diversity initiative is a central component throughout the world of prison ministries and educational programs, responding to fulfill the 'Great Commission.'

Pollsmoor prison in Cape Town, have monthly 'Prayer Walks' where members of various churches get together, walk through the prison cell corridors and pray for the prisoners, lasting for about an hour and a half. As they walk, they touch the prisoner's hands through the bars. During this procession, they hand out Christian booklets. The prison authorities appreciate these prayer walk groups, as they have stated that *'The offenders seem more calm and encouraged, while they experience the love of God, the redemption of Jesus and the presence of the Holy Spirit.'*

In emancipating people from abuse, ignorance, unemployment, poverty and vulnerability, education is deemed the best solution, thus education for offenders is gaining currency in many different countries. It is not only viewed as a human right, but as a foundational stone for equipping offenders to engage in positive rehabilitation and reintegration strategies, as opposed to committing crimes.[35]

5.4 Poverty ex-offenders encounter causing inability to afford education.

Many offender find themselves imprisoned due to theft, because of wanting possessions. Living below the poverty line, they observe with heartache, how others

---

[35] J Sociology Soe, Anth, 3(2): 73-81 (2012) – Downloaded April 2021.

can afford brand name clothing and shoes, gold or silver jewellery, or cars and accessories. The brands they run after are Tommy Hilfiger, Billabong, Nike, Reeboks and Levi, among others. They are often teased and feel left out. Their parents wish they could give their teens all these things, but cannot afford to even feed the family. They are taught by gang members, '*If you have a gun in your hand, you can have anything you want!*' The teens then make the choice to resort to stealing and often the crime goes awry and someone ends up dead (unplanned) changing the offender's life forever.

The average income in offender households is between R500.00 and R5000.00 and education is expensive. The majority of offenders come from extreme poverty backgrounds, often with an absent father or mentor and a mother working two jobs to survive, or alternatively parents who prefer to spend their earnings on abusive substances such as drugs and alcohol, rather than food and education.

With lack of companies willing to employ ex-offenders, as well as the lack of support government offers them, it leaves a gaping hole in any opportunity for free education. The South African Government relies more on Non-Profit or Non-Governmental and Community Based Organisations to assist ex-offenders instead. The ex-offenders lack the technology to type their Curriculum Vitae, then they lack the funds to pay someone else to do it for them. In most cases they do not own identity books and lack funds to obtain one.

They lack funds to own a cell phone or have any airtime, or to ride a taxi to attend an interview. Sadly, without the support of people in the community and their families, ex-offender often have no alternative but to return to crime, for survival. One 'saving grace' they have mastered is that on arrest, they give a false name, as their ID books are not required, they are simply issued a prison number which becomes their identity then on. Once released, their own names are still clear of criminal activity and they lie to cover up their whereabouts for the tears spent in prison.

If the ex-offender made good use of the prison system for educational purposes, his chances of finding employment, are better than those that left prison unchanged.

5.5 Educational challenges children face, in prison and in general society

Many children who find themselves in prison, experience depression and anxiety, as their relatives abandon them. Children are placed into age categories 10 – 14 years old, 14 – 21 years old, 21 – 25 years old.[36] No child under the age of 10 can be prosecuted, thus many children lie about their true age.[37] International

---

[36] The UN Convention on the Rights of the Child (1989) ratified by South Africa in 1995.

[37] The Constitution emphasises the best interests of children, it singles them out for special protection, providing safeguards if in conflict with the law. Child Justice Act

guidelines and the South African Constitution require that children under the age of 18 must be kept separate from adults. Of the prison population of 170,000 inmates at any given time, 1% are children, under 14.

Most prisons in South Africa have school and educational facilities, but many do not.[38] The Department of Correctional Services provides the schools with the materials they need, as well as a library, kept alive from donations by the public.

Prisoners have a low level of literacy and are unfamiliar with discipline and routine, this coupled with lack of motivation makes it difficult to initiate children into an educational culture. No education is provided for unsentenced children of age groups 10 – 14 years old, 14 – 21 years old, 21 – 25 years old. The only schooling education available to children is prison, is ABET.

The DCS places education and training at the heart of its rehabilitation, aimed at removing literacy under qualifications and the absence of critical technical skills and competitions requirements, for employment or self-employment. The education intervention programs were supported by the introduction of a compulsory education policy 2012, aimed at youth up to the age of 25. The DCS has

---

75 of 2008 Section 28 is intended to establish a separate criminal justice system for children who are accused of committing offences.

[38] Child Justice Act 75 of 2008: Section 29 states that everyone has the right to basic education.

presented compulsory education policy to encourage offenders to join education programs.

Early Childhood Development (ECD) programs are slowly being introduced for young children in prison, living in prison cells with their mothers up until age 2.

Children from the age of 8, mostly in African and coloured communities are exposed to the easily available abusive substances, first as an element of fun, then as an element of want and desperate need. The popular social ill substances include Alcohol, Marijuana, Mandrax, Flakka, Krokodil and Tik.
Elderly children and adults, walk around the streets and sell these substances to children. They begin with telling them the substance is like sweets and they sell it cheap, then when the child gets hooked, they sell it at exorbitant prices, causing the child to fall out of school early, being rebellious to their parents, joining gangs, start committing crimes or falling into prostitution and being pimped to pedophiles. The child will do anything to feed their drug habits, soon finding themselves homeless, or as sex slaves, controlled by criminals extorting their bodies for money, or they willingly offer their bodies to strangers for sex in exchange for money for drugs. These children are so vulnerable and are often found murdered by paedophiles, but the crimes go undetected as no-one reports the 'prostitute' missing.

Statistics in South Africa show that the school dropout rate is as high as 56% before reaching matric. As many as 6.5% drop out in Grade 9 already and study later in life through ABET and many never complete their education.[39] Prisons offer ABET and have now made it compulsory for children offenders to attend and complete schooling, while incarcerated, where before the offender had a choice to want to or not. The education levels in prison most prominent are between grade 4 and grade 11. Community centers offer ABET at R200.00 annually for high school dropouts, providing them with all the books needed.

Illiteracy among offenders in all countries, are persons who cannot with understanding read or write a short statement on their everyday life, unable to function effectively nor engage in activities where they cannot even write their own name, or sign their signature, but simply place an 'X' to mark the spot. Sometimes literacy occurs in their mother-tongue, but not in the local universal language, which causes language barriers.

Poverty plays a large role in the abovementioned statistics, but youth getting into the wrong crowd, making bad life choices and poverty are also a contributing factors to dropping out of school. Poverty manifests in many different forms, for instance ill health, undernourishment, deprivation of privileges, informal

---

[39] https://businesstech.co.za/news/government/438509/this-is-the-school-drop-out-rate-in-south-africa/ Article written by staff writer, 6 October 2020 – Downloaded May 2021.

settlement environments, communication and education deficiencies, social status, and increased conflict. Children living in these conditions are disadvantaged, powerless, isolated and very vulnerable.

Education among poverty stricken children is hampered by lack of order in communal structures, lack of hygiene, unsupervised home management, peer pressure and outcomes of this include insecurity, lack of schooling, negative personality construction, a lack of proper orientation in family values, social awkwardness and failure. (Le Roux 1994: 35-36, Engelbrecht 1998: 162-192, Cook 2001, Mohr: 2001).[40]

Educators should not be engaged in the assessment *of* the learner, nor the assessment *of* the learning, but rather their focus should be on assessment *for* the learner. When looking at who seems to be experiencing learning barriers, it is important to first unpack the 'barriers' concept and find ways for learning support, which influences strategies and techniques to overcoming the barriers. The aim of this concept is to understand the child's background, meeting their learning needs and rectifying their deficits to support their future potential and achievements. The concept of overcoming barriers to learning, especially in poor communities, is different to the concept of overcoming lack of assets for learning, such as: Does the child have a desk and chair at home, does the child have their own

---

[40] Addressing Barriers to Learning, A South African Perspective, by Author Emmerentia Landsberg, Published by Schaik Publishers © 2005, Page 28.

room or quiet place to practice and study, does the child have too many chores at home and no time to study, does the child have to look after smaller siblings most of the time, does the child need a laptop, does the child need counselling or therapy, does the child eat at home, does the child have electricity or do they learn by candlelight?

Education is furthermore needed for communities to change their mindsets about welcoming ex-offenders back into communities. For someone who has attended social upliftment programs, studied and educated themselves, will be easier received by the community that someone who stayed a gangster and made no effort to change. Those who attend Christian based educational programs as well, the light and presence of Christ is evident in their attitude and future plans. But while prison offers the security structures of attending these programs weekly, like clockwork, once the offender is in the community, does not have that opportunity anymore, unless they diligently seek it from faith based organisations. On the flip side of the coin, should the ex-offender re-offend, they completely tarnish the trust of the community.

Changing the child's mindset and view of how life is, as opposed to what they have seen and know, is also a challenge. Frequently the child's father, uncle or older brother has been a gangster and prisoner and the child sees them as a mentor or 'hero' and tries to follow in their footsteps.

The church has a mandate to show these children evidence that Jesus Christ should be and is their only mentor and hero, to be followed all the days of their lives.

5.6 Administrative development of Christian educational prison ministry programs, designing and implementing challenges.

Most prisons contain offenders with an assortment of educational backgrounds, levels and experiences. Many may lack basic reading and writing skills, some may have dyslexia and others will have sound literature experience. The experienced offenders usually assist the inexperienced offenders during the attendance of a program. Prisons are willing to provide Christian education to all who seek it.

It is always a good idea to assess offenders upon admission of the first class, for proper evaluation of the pace they need to be taught at, or groups they need to be seated in. Adults who struggle to read and write may be reluctant to attend a program, for fear of embarrassment or being victimised. The Christian educational programs offered, should always promote God's love for his people first and promote the mercy and grace of Jesus Christ and the healing power of the Holy Spirit.

Language could always prove to be a barrier, where possible there should always be a leader present who can interpret, or programs should be translated into different languages to accommodate those who need to understand the content of what is being taught. Some prisoners miss out on attending programs, as they are pre-trial or their sentence is too short to complete it. In this instance, shorter modules or courses, are the answer.

In prison, the spiritual care workers view offenders attending programs as a privilege, based on behavioural patterns, which makes full attendance of all participants at all classes, difficult to expect.

New prison programs should be designed in accordance with the offender's needs, instead of wasting time reinventing the wheel. Programs on making good choices for instance, are a dime a dozen, but a program for necrophilia non-existent. It does not make sense to run a pre-release program, to a group of offenders that have no chance of ever obtaining parole and it has no effect teaching sex-offender programs to offenders who stole a car. The program must validate the environment.

Continuous monitoring of rehabilitation and attitude changes are an important element for prison authorities. Most stakeholders donate money to organisations that run programs that have a proven track record of making a positive and identifiable difference. 'Feel Good Stories' are great, but 'Impact Stories' are much better. With the appropriate program, timeously conducted, targets can be reached in generating fund raising and implementation thereof. An example of such is during COVID another crisis hit at the same time namely Gender Based Violence, and many companies were willing to donate towards this program, yet none so willing to donate towards Anger and Forgiveness Programs. The Department of Correctional Services will also monitor behavioural attitudes and changes, which is vital to the ongoing successful running of the programs. If any program is causing unforeseen problems, such as rioting, encouraging corruption or putting the health and safety of the offender at risk, the Chaplain will put an immediate stop to it.

In order for a newly designed program to be successfully implemented, and evaluation or pilot scheme may be required. This will highlight the objective and outcomes to be achieved. The program must be seen to assist offender's long term, not just be determined as an hour escape out of the prison cell once a week.

5.7 Structuring and designing Christian program content from research, to assist necrophilia and pedophilia:

Rare sexual disorders present challenges, but also opportunities to provide guidance and treatment.

When confronted with disorders that provoke strong emotional or moral responses and are unsupported by programs in place to assist, personal beliefs and biases could influences treatment decisions. Once such example being society will cry out to have the sexual perpetrators castrated or hypnotized! Christians will try to arrange deliverance and counselling. New age or cults may cry out 'anything goes, each one to his own.'

The what, why and how of the perpetrators problem, should form the basis of the intervention.

According to Klara: 2013, one suggestion for educating practitioners is to form clubs that screen films that address these themes. This however, may simply be a desperate attempt for them to understand the disorder.

Since necrophilia and pedophilia are sub-divided into different typologies 'levels' of the disorders, the treatments thereof should be adapted, to the distinction made by the degree of preferential arousal and mental health, as well as levels of deviance and violence applied. It stands to reason that these individuals are complex, with historical and current problems, which contribute toward determining the level of assistance needed.

Assessment:

The purpose of assessment is to gain insight by collecting sufficient information, regarding the perpetrator, to make recommendations for treatment. Information should highlight the mechanisms of the behavioural problem, behaviour prior to and after the crime has been committed, which includes risk assessment, historical abuse and personality assessments. Most pedophiles and necrophiles have their own 'signature' methods of crime, similar to that of serial killers, examples being the Station Strangler, the ABC Killer, Jack the Ripper, Jeffrey Dahmer (Murder with Cannibalism), Ted Bundy, Mortimar Saunders, Pedro Lopez (Killed over 300 children). Treatment has to be adapted to the misconduct and behaviour patterns.

Identifying the problem:

Case formulation should begin with face-to-face interviews with the offender and perhaps extend interviews with their close friends, work associates and family members. A full psychological assessment needs to be established.

Engaging the offender:

It is essential that the case worker conducting the interview with the offender, is well qualified, educated, trained and competent to do so. Best practices need to be applied, engaging in a manner that the offender opens up and feels 'understood' and not judged by the interviewee. The case worker should be warm, and yet straightforward in their line of questioning style, with open ended questions to provoke increase in information. Asking the right questions is crucial. An open ended question example would be, 'Tell me what transpired, I am really curious to hear the particulars of your story.'

Risk assessment:

A comfort level should be experienced between case worker and offender. A useful framework of questions can be researched from different sources: (Hanson & Thornton, 2000; Helmus, Thornton, Hanson, & Babchishin, 2012), Hare Psychopathy Checklist–Revised (Hare, 1991, 2003)[41], giving a wide variety of personality and behavioural variables relevant to these sexual crimes and psychosocial functioning. The case worker is to provide a safe-space for the offender to feel free to talk.

In some cases the offender may distort the truth 'for want of fame,' minimise aspects of their crimes 'for want of sympathy' or inadvertently lie 'the privacy is the personal fantasy that must be kept secret.'

Mental illness, substance abuse, past physical or sexual abuse, past animal abuse or mutilation, past satanic worship in their ancestry, overbearing mothers, absent fathers, lack of schooling, in other cases above

---

[41] In Press, L. Mellor, A. Aggrawal, & E. Hickey (Eds.), Necrophilia: A global anthology, Andrew E. Brankley

average intelligence, etc. are broad coding criteria to be explored.

Precipitant origins provide information on events that trigger the offender's behaviour, such as trains of thought, physical sensations, feelings, rejection, traumatic treatment from others, witnessing killing or skinning of animals, witnessing abuse as a child, being a victim of abuse, or harsh and domineering words spoken over their lives. These origins will provide intervention target treatments.

Crime scene analysis:

Details of the crimes committed by the perpetrators can be obtained from various sources, police records, court transcripts, newspaper articles, dissertation research and libraries. The crime scene information helps to establish the extent, severity, scope and rate of reoccurrence of their problematic behaviour patterns. In order for these sexual disorders to be properly diagnosed, there has to be evidence that it has taken place over a prolonged period of time. A demonstration of this would be a necrophile that is sexually aroused by drinking blood, or pre/post mortem acts of torture or mutilation as a method of humiliating the victim; or a paedophile that is sexually aroused by stealing little girl's panties off wash lines; so as not be caught actually molesting children, thus keeping their fantasy private.

Treatment:

According to (Martinson: 1974) current efforts to identify effective means of treating these sexual offenders, arose to early reactions that 'nothing works.' (Andrews & Bonta, 1998; Hanson, Bourgon, Helmus, & Hodgson, 2009; Hanson & Yates: 2013) promote the RNR Model: Risk, Needs and Responsivity. Common responses to treatment include cognitions regarding sexuality, emotion regulation, relationship challenges and sexual deviance.[42] These programs however are incomplete, as they focus on behavioural patterns as opposed to treating multi-faceted targets.

While necrophilia and pedophilia invoke intense emotional reactions from forensic, pathological and anthropological professionals, as well as community members, a thorough guide treatment and management of such individuals, is crucial.

Bringing God into the equation is debateable by different people groups.

---

[42] Beech and Ward: 2004, Marshall: 2011.

Chapter 6   MENTORSHIP EDUCATION

6.1 Effects of fatherlessness, educating offenders through mentors as stand-ins.

'I was important in the life of a child.' ~Kevin Rosnover

The word 'mentor' refers to wise advisor, trusted counsellor, coach, host, teacher, exemplar, guide and friend. Jesus is a perfect example to follow, as he had all these qualities. A mentor is usually an older, more experienced person who seeks to further develop that character and competence of a younger person, by instilling complex skills and traits in which the mentor is already efficient. The guidance is accomplished through instruction, demonstration, building a trust based relationship encouragement and challenge over an extended period of time. During the process, the mentor and mentee develop a special bond with mutual commitment, loyalty and respect and assists the mentee to find their true identity in Christ.

The expression 'mentor' is not used in the bible, but the concept of it is written and portrayed throughout the Old and New Testaments:

- Abraham was a mentor to Lot
- Moses was a mentor to Joshua
- Naomi was a mentor to Ruth
- Eli was a mentor to Samuel
- Barnabus was a mentor to Paul

- Elizabeth was a mentor to Mary
- Elijah was a mentor to Elisha
- Priscilla and Aquila were mentors to Apollos
- Paul was a mentor to Timothy
- Jesus was a mentor to his disciples

In the past, the mentee has usually experienced the following cycle of disruption:

- Bad and untrustworthy information
- Lies
- Bad advice and instructions
- Broken trust
- Non-godly advice or guidance
- Responses motivated by anger, fear and pain
- Disruptive attitude, mentality and behaviour
- Easily influenced by peer pressure
- No respect for adults correction or teaching
- Broken family environment
- Dysfunctional life patterns
- Destructive behaviour
- Lack of purpose, interest
- A hatred for authority
- Anger
- Lack of identity
- Emotionally, physically and spiritually damaged
- Failure complex
- Do not trust adults easily
- Unmet needs
- Abuse (but not in all cases)
- Neglect (but not in all cases)

- Avoid responsibility and consequences of bad behaviour
- Lack of guidance in making good choices

Role models and mentors are imperative in every sphere of leadership, especially prison ministry leadership. In prisons for example, role models and mentors stand in the gap for 'absent fathers' and in turn, those prisoners that are positively impacted result in reduced recidivism and stopping the cycle, by changing their ways and becoming better fathers. Through this, families and the wider community are positively affected.

The dynamics of how the mentoring is carried out also matters, it is better for the mentor to sit next to the mentee, not opposite them, keeping eye contact is important yet keeping healthy space and of course, maintaining boundaries. Mentoring should be conducted in a safe space and common ground area, with the understanding that mentees contacting mentors during 'family time hours' are not allowed. Boundaries are also important if the mentee is one sex and the mentor another, as mentees are vulnerable but can also be somewhat manipulative, and mentors too. For some mentees that have no proper family structure, they can quickly see the mentor as the stand-in of a mother or father figure, instead of seeing God as their Father and 'go-to' in all things. This could have precarious and sad consequences.

Mentoring is choosing to focus your attention on someone who has lost their way and lived a 'fatherless' life, possibly in despondency, having also given up on their dreams. The majority of prisoners in South Africa come from dysfunctional homes. Society sees the prisoner as lost, however God sees the 'lost' mentee as someone of purpose, plan and promise. The mentoring journey offers many rewards for mentor and mentee alike, it is truly a fulfilling and empowering experience. A structured and trusted relationship develops confidence, competence and character in the mentee.

Some of the mentor's responsibilities should include:

- Attentive listening to the mentee (do not be distracted)
- Keep confidences and stay confidential (do not break the mentee's trust)
- Be a mature Christian, who is in relationship with God
- Rely on the Holy Spirit (to help you hear and see things not being said by the mentee)
- Rely on the Holy Spirit, to help you know how to respond to the mentee
- Be a person of integrity, non-biased, non-judgemental
- Be able to redirect the mentee to someone else more qualified to deal with the problems, if you are not equipped to do so (do not let pride stand in the way of the mentee's healing and spiritual; growth)

- Encourage the mentee to journal and track his progress
- Give your mentee responsibilities to carry out
- If you feel mismatched as a mentor to your mentee, swop

'They don't care about how much you know, until they know how much you care.'~ Quote Theodore Roosevelt

Although mentoring is not a process of 'one size fits all' because the dynamics change based on differences: males and females, age groups, races and cultures, etc. Mentoring is one of the most beneficial ways to impact 'at-risk' youth. Those youth who have a mentor, have lower incidences of drug use, violent behaviour, less likely to commit crimes, improved social skills, enhanced self-esteem, less recidivism effect, enriched self-confidence and a sense of belonging, and if the mentor is a trustworthy Christian, the mentee will follow a Godly path.

Factors to consider when mentoring are: Who raised the mentee? What role did their father / mother play? Were they separated from your siblings? If not raised by parents, where were their parents? If others took care of them, how did they treat them? Do their parents pay attention to them or ignore them? Were they rejected before they were born? Were they an unwanted baby? Were they adopted? Do they think they have a problem controlling their anger? Are they able to forgive all that was wrongfully done to them? Did adults break their trust? Are the parents of the mentee addicted to substances?

A mother nurtures, while a father establishes identity. An absent father creates a void that is difficult to fill if the mentee does not have the fulfillment of Christianity. Mentoring is a blessing! A mentoring leader must set and be an example and role model of what he is encouraging the mentee offender to be.

6.2 Gangsterism as a false family structure.

Prisoners, especially from a fatherless home, feel fear of the unknown and not knowing what to expect when the prison gate gets slammed shut for the first time and they hear the clanging sound of the keys locking them in. Immediately, if they are placed in a shared cell, they could have up to 20 pairs of eyes staring at them as they make their way to the available stretcher for a bed. Some will whistle, some will make rude remarks, some will walk up to them with keen sexual interest and some will either intimidate them, laugh at them or ignore them. Either way, it's a moment frozen in time, vulnerable and fearful, for the new recruit.

On beginning to make their bed, they will be further threatened, or shouted at from the other side of the room, to 'sleep with one eye open.' A person paralyzed by fear, will compromise or do whatever it takes to make the fear disappear.

That is the moment, the gang member or leader will step in and offer protection, with the false perception that the 'gang' will be his/her new 'family.' Some prisoners have no choice but to embark on gay sexual acts, for fear of losing their lives. This puts them at risk of HIV / Aids. The gang becomes a defense protection mechanism and a source of provision, for anything the offender needs.

God designed a family, father, mother and children. The devil comes to distort God's original design, by breaking up the family and the best way to achieve this, is to remove the father out of the family circle. In this way, the children grow up with no identity, no mentoring and no discipline. The gangs offer the prisoner a false perception of family, further destroying them, whereas God wants to add them to His family and heal them.

6.3 Preparing men and women to become professional educators in prison environments.

There are rules of the roads, in homes, ministry, schools and rules in prisons. Above all rules of any prison ministry organisations, ***prison rules rule!*** Nothing can be done, or taken into prison without the permission of the Prison Head and Spiritual Care Worker.

God has a special place in his heart for prison ministry leaders and although prisons know the offenders by numbers, God knows them by name.

Prison ministry leaders should obtain professional training for educating offenders, (a challenging people group) as well as register with a Christian governing body. Always respect the team leader and follow God's calling and vision for the ministry. All prison ministry leaders must be screened, be in a personal relationship with God, be confidential, be non-judgmental and have a testimony to share. Leaders should not get too emotionally attached to the offenders and also be open to learning from the offenders.

Leaders and educators in prisons, need to be organized and have their lessons prepared in advance, as well as all the necessary training materials and stationary, (with preceding permission from the prison Head). Offenders can tell when a lesson was not well prepared. Leaders should always arrive on time at the prison and respect the allocated time given for the lesson. They should always pray, putting on the armour of God before entering prison, pray before the lesson begins and again when the lesson ends. They need to be sensitive to and allow the Holy Spirit to lead the lesson and put man's agenda aside.

When teaching in prisons, there will always be loud noise and many distractions, awareness of gang activity and possible passing around of contraband. Offenders are easily distracted and there are many different personality types represented per classroom, thus lessons need to be interesting and age appropriate. Leaders to stay focused on the topic of the lesson of the day and make the classes interactive. Unity is key - it is imperative that teams of prison ministry leaders stay bonded and meet regularly, as offenders quickly pick up on division or disagreements among leaders. Rather sort out disagreements off the prison premises. Different ministries have different teaching methods, leaders find the simplest and most effective and build on that model.

Research and statistics of the prisons ministered in should be well known to prison ministry leaders, in order to run appropriate programs for the offenders being ministered to. Open communication with the Spiritual Care Worker is important to determine which underlying problems are experienced by the prison authorities, regarding the offender's behaviour patterns as well as the challenges the offenders will face in the community once released. The correct offenders attending the program needs to be discussed with the Spiritual Care Worker, to ensure the program being run is aimed at the targeted audience. It is no use running sexual offenders course with offenders that only stole a loaf of bread.

Leaders should always remind offenders that counselling is available.

6.4 Training up disciples through Christian education.

One of God's most prominent commands mandates us to obey the calling of 'The Great Commission.' Through Christian education, we can teach each other to grow as members of the body of Christ, to obey God and to follow Jesus. Disciples must know God to teach about God, for a blind man cannot lead another blind man.[43]

Without a mentor, or father figure, it is difficult for a person to establish their identity in Christ. It is crucial for the church to equip and train disciples, as we shall not live forever, but God's word and ministry will go on. Discipleship courses can assist secular class learners to think further than just academic outcomes, as God's wisdom will give them purpose and a meaningful life. Motivating and guiding backsliders, helping our communities heal and true evangelism and mission derive from disciples answering God's call.

6.5 Learning shaping love

Recent studies conducted by (Smith: 2009, 2013, 2016b) intrinsically link learning and love in a vitally different manner, interrupting traditional approaches to Christian education by suggesting change of focus to shaping and forming ones loves or desires. At the heart of this adage that every pedagogy assumes an

---

[43] Train Disciple Makers, Published by Nehemiah Bible Institute, by Author Dr. Hennie van Deventer, Pages 8-18.

understanding of what it means to be human. How do Christian educators analyse people? Smith reminds us that in the 11th century, the universities invited people into a way of life to make them lovers of God who desired to learn, to impact the world around them and teach others to love God. He claims that to be human is to love and what we love, determines who we are. (Anderson: 2014) added education becomes the process of learning to love the right things and gaining the knowledge to love what God loves, so we can reflect who he is and what he does.

Smith links humans with Aristotle and Augustine, identifying three main factors:

- We are made for something, God made us on purpose, for a purpose, we are made in his image and need to love God and ourselves.

- The centre of the human person is the heart, the heart is our seat of loves and longings. Educationally we are to learn to understand what the heart loves and to find perfect rest in God.

- Every creature created by God is a loving creature, with loves and desires. You learn to love by practise. Augustine challenges in his book, asking us the questions: How do I learn to love and how does my heart get aimed?

Public learning creates two chronicles: The existence of shared narratives and the capacity to provide a stimulated reason for schooling and learning. As humans we underestimate the extent to which our desires have been co-opted by secular learning that has trained us to love other gods and what they have to offer us. Education teaches us not to do the same thing differently, but to rather do something different altogether, his argument being radical and holistic Christian education as the 'something different.' Biblical views gives students new and practical approaches. While the Christian educator counsels and teaches out of who they are, should counsel and teach in accordance with and through the lens of who the student is, 'In Christ's image.'

Christian education is for lovers as well as for deep thinkers and in this sense a life-long vocation for students that passionately desire to study to fittingly bear the image of God for and to the world, so all may flourish. Well known (Professor of Philosophy, Arthur Frank Holmes: 1987) encourages the question to not ask one-self about Christian education, 'What am I doing with it?' but rather, 'What is it doing for and to me, as a person?' Education's purpose is to make one a 'whole' person, which shows that theoretically and practically, education is beneficial and engages not just the hands, but the head and the heart too.

Ironically, how we see people, is how we see God and in turn, how we see God, is how we see people, which shapes how important or worthy, we think education is. Christian education helps us better understand humans and better understand God.

Christian education offers thought provoking commixture of reading, reflection, meditation, inspiration, imagination and in the passionate pursuit of it, a great love for God.[44]

---

[44] Reimagining Christian Education, book by Johannes M. Leutz, Tony Dowden and Beverley Norsworthy, Published by Springer, Singapore © 2018, Pages 5 - 9.

Chapter 7   RECIDIVISM AND REHABILITATION

7.1 Define recidivism and rehabilitation.

Recidivism:

According to (Winnicott 1984:123) recidivism is defined as an offender's inclination to repeat their criminal activity, despite efforts of reformation and far too many ex-offenders establish themselves in productive, crime free lives after release. Criminologists study the 'why' criminals behave the way they do, what their motives are, their social conditions, their political ideology and current friendship circles. These studies are imperative to determine and understand factors that influence behaviour patterns, for more effective methods to reduction recidivism.

Rehabilitation:

Refers to the process of retraining those who committed crime, which includes educational skills, with the goal to reintegrate offenders back into society. One of the challenges inmates face, is being institutionalised, living in prison for so long, they forget how normal life on the outside functions. Through this, they often reoffend to go back to the 'security' of prison. The lack of education has two influences, it can cause poverty and contribute to crimes being committed.

Reintegration and rehabilitation remain one of the prison institution's greatest challenges, as the effectiveness thereof is crucial in combatting recidivism.

7.2 Statistics of recidivism in South African prisons.

Refers to the rate or extent at which prisoners re-offend. There is no official government department that maintains these figures, as the numbers include those outside of prison as well as inside of prison. A consistent measurement is lacking. Some research has been conducted by civil society and academics on a small scale and the results only provide estimates of the recidivism rate, as 87%.[45] However, careful consideration should be taken into account before the recidivism rate is expressed, such as: age groups, ethnic groups, gang activity groups and the number of times the same person has been back to prison.

Not enough research or monitoring of recidivism rates are evident, although it is an economic pandemic, as the state spends money on security, justice, correctional and rehabilitation systems. Although an important exploration of study, very little information is available on recidivism rates. (Kofi Poku Quan-Balfour and Britta E. Zawada: 2012) surmise that the recidivism rates could be as high as 95%, yet official figures are unknown.

---

[45] https://mg.co.za/article/2020-01-17-revolving-door-of-crime-and-jail/

There is a dire need, thus an effective structure should be put in place, with one central monitoring body, to accurately calculate recidivism rates in South Africa.

7.3 Rehabilitation of children in prison.

Few prisons in South Africa offer social work or rehabilitation programs to children aged 9 to 24. On conducting research, Anne McKay (MA Clinical Psychologist) suggested that for awaiting trial children, these rehabilitation programs could be introduced:

- Sexual education and HIV prevention
- Substance abuse
- Conflict resolution
- Life skills training
- Career guidance
- Educational counselling
- Economic alternatives to crime
- Street law
- Legal education
- Fostering personal responsibility
- Active decision making
- Community involvement

Interestingly, nowhere on her comprehensive list, does Anne McKay suggest Christian education, as a manner of rehabilitation.

The majority of prisons in South Africa endorse Christian education and volunteers ministries. What difference does Christianity make to rehabilitation? According to NICRO specific Christianity roles and spiritual belief systems do play direct and unique roles in predicting rehabilitation outcomes whereas 'religious' activity do not. Notably, a self-reported individual connection to God is an extremely robust predictor, of both subjective and objective outcomes.

Opportunities for rehabilitation of children in prison exist through schooling education, prison ministry organisation programs, counselling, in prison activities and discipline procedures. The churches goal should not be only for children to know the bible, or to behave in certain Christian ways, but to know, love and walk with God, in order to grow into mature people of faith, as Christian education should be deemed 'God's Curriculum,' not mans.[46]

An evidence based plan needs to be implemented to turn lives around, in large by restoring the link between people who offend and those who care what happens to them. A guiding principle is that supportive connections help ex-offenders to prevent reoffending and those connections should start in the neighbourhoods where youth are most susceptible to crime.

---

[46] Introduction to Christian Education and Formation, book by Ronald T. Habermas (Published by Zondervan) © 2009, Pages 151-161.

Children under 12 must be proved mentally stable enough according to their age, before being tried. They will first go to a mental health institution for evaluation, as they may have a mental disorder. Depression and anxiety plays a role, even in children that could have resulted from an accumulation of negative events or disappointments, traumatic events, the loss of a loved one or parents that practise substance abuse, peer pressure and sexual abuse. Mood disorders vary vastly between adults and children. Boys tend to be more aggressive and girls passive.

Some children criminals have been found to be demonised and needed deliverance.

Children incarcerated with their mothers, up to age 2:

Just as lack of physical care and nurturing can lead to poor health or death, lack of social nurturing produced distorted emotional development and will stunt intellectual growth. Poor nutrition during infancy has lifelong detrimental effects. Just as important as nutrition is, socialization and affection for physical needs is. In World War II, children that were fed, bathed, clothed and given medical attention, lacked love and nurturing of their mothers as they were only handled briefly daily by busy nurses.

The majority of these children could not walk, talk or stand by age 4, and some had become mentally retarded. Without proper stimulation, love, gentle discipline and care for children up until the age of 2, that are incarcerated with their mothers, the babies become underdeveloped, undernourished and prefer social isolation in adulthood.[47]

Children by socially conventional standards, should be given access to a structured daily program, involving at least four hours a day of education and social interaction, exercise, adequate books and study materials. More effort should be made to introduce Early Childhood Development (ECD) in female prisons, as opposed to television viewing all day for stimulation.

Children are vulnerable and the psychological emotional effect on the mother and child, when the toddler turns 2, is extremely traumatic. All the child has known until then, is the confines of the prison cell nursery and its mother and then all the child's security gets stripped away on its second birthday. Not having the same educational opportunities as babies on the outside of prison, with toys and puzzle building and other stimulants, starts life from a somewhat disadvantaged point, not to mention the emotional suffering of separation anxiety.

---

[47] Introduction to Psychology and Counselling, Christian Perspectives and Applications, book by Paul D. Meier, Frank B. Minirth, Frank B. Wichern and Donald E. Ratcliff (Published by Baker Books) © Second Edition 2000, Pages 186-198.

The child and mother are left to the mercy of people on the outside taking care of the child, to bring the child to prison from time to time to visit the mother and each time the child goes home after an hour visit, the trauma is relived.

Prison ministry volunteers should be given regular opportunities to minister to little children with storytelling, as well as play games to stimulate them. Basic lessons in childhood will leave their mark throughout life, not only in basic manner towards social norms, but in their ability to navigate receiving love and love in turn, fosters its own lasting biological and educational footprints.

7.4 Rehabilitation of adults in prison.

Some rehabilitation programs for adults that would be effective, to assist them after release, would include skills and trades such as:

- Skills development
- Carpentry
- Plumbing
- Painting
- Shoe and handbag repairs
- Watch repairs
- Car repairs
- Electrical appliance repairs
- Sewing
- Baking bread

- Brick-laying
- Gardening
- Farming
- Radio presenting
- Motivational Speaker
- Facilitating HIV / Aids Courses
- Facilitating First Aid Courses
- Health and occupational safety
- Facilitating theology / ministry courses
- Entrepreneurial skills
- Life skills
- Social skills
- Employment readiness
- Art classes
- Security guard work
- Beadwork
- Community development, gang awareness, drug awareness talks at schools
- Literature
- Sports

More research and diligence is needed when training offenders for vocational skills, as it also depends on their work geographical environment and home environment, the aim should be to tease out what will be available and what works best. A meta-analysis is a comprehensive manner to ascertain multiple studies to develop consensus about the efficiency and effectiveness of the intervention or educational program.

Through prison education, former prisoners become lawyers in South Africa

Is such redemption possible, that secular education can turn offenders into lawyers?

If an ex-offender has a criminal record and were to apply for a position in a legal profession, they would hope to be successful in being accepted. However, a moral character flaw would lead the application to fail. The criminal record is a challenging obstacle and such applications may only succeed in exceptional circumstances, as hope alone is insufficient. Before anyone can be tried for a criminal offence, they must be able to comprehend the charges against them and to assist with their own defence.

The Attorney Act 53 of 1979 as amended lists the requirements to be complied with in order to qualify for and be admitted as an attorney in South Africa (SA). They must prove that they are 21 or older, a lawful SA citizen and has the minimum stipulated academic qualifications, SAPS clearance, as well as being a fit and proper person to be admitted as an attorney. Each application is dealt with based on its merits. The first time criminal record applicant, has a weighty burden to convince the court that they are fit for the legal profession.

In view of the above Act, lawyers that derived from studying in prison consist of political ex-prisoners, termed as 'honourable motives,' not murderers or heinous crimes criminals, namely Krause, Mandela, Moseneke and Matthews.[48]

International attorneys that defend criminals of sexual crimes

The USA legal system says 'better than one innocent man wrongfully incarcerated, rather let ten guilty men go.'

Society judges lawyers who defend criminals that have committed heinous crimes, however the world needs lawyers who can defend the cases of the most despised people in the world. Professor Alan Dershowitz and Attorney Bobbi C. Sternheim are a typical examples, as he has taken on cases that no one else was willing to, such as Donald Trump, Hillary and Bill Clinton, Jeffrey Epstein, John Adams, Leon Black, all of which are suspected on charges of pedophilia in association with Jeffrey Epstein and Ghislaine Maxwell.

Richard Lawson, Kimberley A. Berry, Sarah Gheesling, Gabriel Winters and David R.T. Hearth employed at Richard Lawson Attorneys defend criminals, in the areas of enticing children for indecent proposals, failure to register as a sex offender, incest,

---

[48] M Slabbert BA (Hons) HED BProc LLB LLD (UFS) Professor Department of Jurisprudence University of South Africa, 2011 "The requirement of being a 'Fit and Proper' person for the legal profession."

internet sex crimes, and possession of child pornography, statutory rape, child molestation, aggravated child molestation, bestiality and necrophilia.

Lawyer Gerry Boyle defended Jeffrey Dahmer, famous paedophile, necrophile, cannibal and sadist.

7.5 Forgiveness, healing offenders and victims.

Forgiveness as education:

(Enright, Knuston, Holter, Baskin: 2007) have scientifically tested forgiveness curricula for adolescents and children, and discovered that without forgiveness as education another person may easily associate forgiving and reconciling as one thing and stay in an abusive relationship. With forgiveness education, forgiveness is possible, reconciliation and emotional healing can take place.

Education is incomplete until educators fold into it the basic strategies to overcoming severe injustices that students, once they become adults, can say 'I was given room to learn how to forgive.'

It is unfortunate that educational institutions fail to make forgiveness a natural part of life through early education. This would prevent and empower adolescents and children from being crushed by other's cruelty.[49]

Consider if God said this to a victim:

'What if they would beg for my forgiveness? What if they would realise that they are unable to go back and change the past, but would then decide not to allow the past to determine their future any longer? What if they would say sorry and would live with the pain of regret for what they have done to you? Am I to favour only your prayer and not consider theirs, or do you think I should consider both sides?

What if they have *never* repented to me for what they have done to you? Do I have a right to expect you to forgive them anyway? If you choose to forgive them, it will set you free from the chains that bind you, chains that are holding you prisoner.

The only way you are going to let go of that anger, is through forgiveness.'

Consider if God said this to an offender:

'They may reject you and not forgive you for what you have done, but that will be a matter between myself and them. Do not be overcome by the fear of what will happen, simply because they choose not to forgive you.

---

[49] Psychology Today Magazine, Article written by Robert Enright Ph.D. called The Forgiving Life, Why we need forgiveness education – Downloaded April 2021.

I will work in their hearts, but in the meantime, learn to forgive yourself.'

Think about the spider's excellent example of being fearless. Imagine it has just spun a huge well-designed web in a corner, taking a lot of time and effort to build. But when it is destroyed, the spider does not sit in a heap on the floor and cry. It does not feel sorry for itself and take a few days off for trauma counselling nor does it go and bite the housewife to justify the unfairness of it all.

Nothing good comes from negative thinking, limitations or fear. The spider might have lost everything, but it does not hate the lady, nor does it go around gossiping about her to all the other spiders. The spider harbours no unforgiveness in its heart and does not blame anyone for its misfortune. It simply walks to the next corner and starts rebuilding! It is really a very special creature. I had fun creating it. You are a special creature too. I lovingly made you with the ability to forgive, because I forgave you first.

Now, go and apologise and ask forgiveness, but even if they decide that they will never forgive you, have the assurance that I do.'

The mask of unforgiveness:

The longer we wear our masks, the more comfortable they feel. How do we remove these masks to live as God requires? If you had to put a plastic mask over your face and wear it day in and day out, it would make you hot and bothered. Breathing would not be easy, seeing properly would not be easy, speaking may also prove to be more difficult. We need to shed the masks we wear if we want to be free. Free to be real. So we can conclude that wearing masks can cause us to become very lonely people. We have to start by looking to God and looking at our inner selves.

Many people quote the bible verse as 'resist the devil and he will flee' but the whole verse says, 'seek God first, then resist the devil and he will flee.' Without God we do not have the strength to overcome challenges like removing our masks, in a way that heals us completely. Being honest with God and yourself is the way to remove the mask. God will help you, but he is quietly waiting for you to make the decision and to ask him to do so.

'Our lives only improve when we are willing to take chances and the first and most difficult risk we can take, is to be honest with ourselves.' ~ Quote Walter Anderson.

How easy is it to let go? Especially if we have experienced pain, regret, guilt, failure, rejection and unforgiveness. Forgiveness is the key to letting go.

Forgiveness of those we hurt, forgiveness of ourselves for pain we caused and forgiveness towards those who caused us pain and distress. Masks encourage us to seek the approval of others, instead of seeking God's approval. No matter what others think of us or say about us, we always have God's approval so we need to live a life that is pleasing to him.

Behind every mask there is a face and behind every face there is a story. There are many faces that mask themselves as love, but they truthfully lack the attributes that love possesses or depicts. Love is not love unless it costs something and love is not love unless it leads to freedom.

How easy is forgiveness?

What do we fear will happen if we choose to forgive? We should not be afraid to ask ourselves the right questions about our worth, our thoughts, our purpose and our emotions. Our self-esteem is based on Christ dying for us, not on the things man uses to measures us. God has made us in his image, so our value lies in who we know, not what we do. God loves us unconditionally and sent his Son Jesus to die for our sins and through that, redeems us.

We need not walk in shame, we can merely ask God to forgive anything we have done. We are able to forgive others, as forgiveness is a choice. Christ forgave us first, giving us the strength and ability to forgive others and ourselves.

It is not easy to forgive, however it is possible to forgive someone who has continually abused you, it is in fact a necessary step to moving on.

7.6 Letting go of the victim mentality through Christian educational programs.

What is a victim mentality?

Some people view a victim mentality as a way of seeking and receiving attention, pity or pleasure, which psychologists call a 'secondary gain.' This term means that by not solving a problem, could have many benefits. The person with a victim mentality also feels satisfaction or a thrill, by creating a sense of guilt for others and refusing to accept responsibility. The victim that continually holds onto the problem, could be manipulative or damaging to the perpetrator, making them pay by reminding them and instilling fear, guilt of being exposed, or giving them a sense of *you owe me, because of what you did!* In this instance, the victim becomes the victimiser.

Our greatest trump card to overcoming fears of any kind, is the Holy Spirit and God's word, as his power transforms fear to perfect peace, even when we do not understand it. It also uproots the lies planted in our hearts by the enemy and brings us back into God's will, which is 'do not fear!'

What are the dangers of a victim mentality?

The victim's chronic pessimistic outlook could irritate and wear down their friends, colleagues, family members and even counsellor or pastor. A victim mentality slows down production in their workplace, people start to avoid them and never invite them over, which is damaging to all their relationships. This type of victim, most likely does not wish to receive any help and will react negatively to any attempts to change their behaviour or mind-set and may even turn on the helper, accusing them of causing further stress.

Individuals with victim mentalities, often blame their ills and misfortunes on someone or something else and have a distorted view that the problem have permanence. The victim may often lie and twist the facts, to bring their point across. They also display dysfunctional dynamics, such as crying wolf, thus losing credibility and having people ignore their concerns – because no one knows what is legitimately truth or not.

There is a fine line between victimisation and oppression.

Victim mentality thought patterns include

- 'I give up'
- 'It does not matter what I do, nothing will help'
- 'I have no control over the outcome'
- 'I have stopped trying'
- 'I feel overwhelmed all the time' (for years already)

- 'I lost the struggle and I feel helpless'
- 'I feel my actions are futile, so I feel there is no hope'
- 'I feel so isolated and victimised' (they are isolating themselves)
- 'My role in life is to be a loser'
- 'I shouldn't complain, but …'

The difference between being a martyr and a victim

- Martyrs often realise they are being taken advantage of and choose to remain in the situation. Victims do not realise they are being taken advantage of or treated unfairly, but others see it clearly, so they have a choice to remain in the situation or not, however if they choose to stay, they risk becoming a martyr.
- Martyrs know their rights, but victims have their rights ignored by the abused.
- Martyrs seek sympathy as they seem stuck in their plight. Victims hardly ever seek help
- Martyrs believe it is their obligation to stay in their situation, feeling guilty if they let go. Victims want change and are usually desperate for solutions.
- Martyrs rarely change their tales of woe and will still be experiencing the same fate as when you spoke to them a long time ago. Victims seek help and are more apt to coming out of their situation.

- Martyrs mask their behaviour and attitude, usually fooling themselves. Victims are usually open and honest about their discomfort and willingly seek advice or healing.

Overcoming a victim mentality

One of the first symptoms of victim mentality is their low self-esteem which needs rebuilding as well as breaking their own cycle of isolation. Moving them away from the *'why me?'* way of thinking, to only the *'why?'* Some may be pursuing justice, of which conducting public speaking, launching an anti-violence campaign or giving testimonies on different platforms, is a way out of being overly defensive, by rather raising awareness and embracing freedom. In this way, feelings of fear and anger are transformed into constructive social interaction, thus also helping others in that situation.

There are many victims who have positively affected the law, by either putting a new law in place or changing an existing one for future victims to benefit. Although they may become activists, it still does not replace the healing that comes with counselling as they need to work through their emotions, thus activism should be viewed as a support, not a solution.

Activism should also be cautioned in that the victim may feel they are being exploited or the victim could possibly start exploiting others through these campaigns.

The victim's involvement, should benefit themselves and be part of community effort improvement. By taking on these new roles and responsibilities, victims improve their self-esteem, advance their recovery and feel they have more control over their lives, while realising they have something significant and valuable to contribute.

South Africa has a 16 days of activism for victims of crime and the abused annually every June, where various NPO's and activists take part in campaigns to raise awareness and assist victims.

7.7 Letting go of anger through Christian educational programs

Educational programs run in prison should include anger management. Anger causes prisoners to showcase aggressive behavioural patterns and be less controllable by prison officials. Programs on anger significantly lower recidivism.[50]

---

[50] https://www.ojp.gov/ncjrs/virtual-library/abstracts/anger-management-prison-evaluation-anger-management-program

What should be taught about letting go of anger, is that the root of anger is fear, hurt, rejection, injustice, frustration, pressure and when ones future feels threatened. Anger is a strong emotion that could be used to your advantage or disadvantage. The three doors to anger are thought, word and deed. Anger is a powerful emotion that can cause you to make a decision on the spur of the moment that can detrimentally affect the rest of your life. Anger in itself, can hold you prisoner, keeping you in a place of unforgiveness, towards yourself and others.

Your past or present circumstances could cause you to be angry, because many things in life seem unfair. Yet you could also be angry at a stupid choice you made, something you did, that you are not able to undo. Being angry at yourself, at others or at God is one method the devil uses to hold you in bondage, preventing you from being free in Christ. Being angry could make you feel that you are not good enough for God to love you.

A few examples of what sparks your anger in prison, are when someone insults your mother, steals your things, someone else was disobedient but you also got punished, someone gossips about you, the gang threatens you, people criticise or judge you, nobody listens to you and the authorities rudely tell you what to do.

Steps to control anger include listening to calming music, walking away, instead of fighting, remaining silent instead of saying something you will regret, apologising to the person you hurt, forgiving and talking about it to someone you can trust.

Ways to combat anger are to forgive quickly *(Matthew 18:22)*, pray *(Psalm 37:7-8)*, practice self-control *(Ephesians 4:26-27)*, write down your feelings, make peace, do not hold a grudge *(Matthew 5:21-26)*.

Letting anger go is a personal choice, as no one can decide to do it on your behalf *(James 1:19-20)* and respect is earned, but it cannot be earned from a point of anger. Friends may play a joke on you which could make you angry, simply because they are not aware of your past circumstances. So stay calm and forgive quickly. There will always be battles that you will not be strong enough to overcome. However, you can ask God to heal your hurt and give you the grace to forgive, so that you will be able to practise self-control and let go of anger.

7.8 The impact of employment or non-employment, versus entrepreneurship

Prison ministries and mentors play an integral role in delivering Christian education inside prison for sentenced offenders and outside of prison for ex-offenders.

The importance of religious organisations cannot be ignored in how it affects behavioural changes and attitudes, however is it enough to assist the offender on release from prison, to find employment, or even acceptance and forgiveness from family and community members?

Unemployment is one of the largest socio-economic challenges that South Africans face. The percentage thereof differs from province to province, but overall the unemployment rate is 32.5% after a year of COVID, which equates to 7.2 Million people that have little or no income.[51] The unemployment rate is calculated by adding the amount of people in the labour force, then dividing it by the total adult population and multiplying by 100 to effect the correct %.

While there are organisations that assist ex-offenders with clothing, food and general basic needs, the need for employment and becoming independent to regain their dignity, remains. Men principally, have the perception that they are the 'providers' for the family, especially in certain cultures and find it difficult to adjust on the outside without being employed.

---

[51] https:// www.news24.com / fin24/economy / sas-jobless-grows-to-72-million-as-unemployment-rate-breaches-new-record- 20210223 - downloaded April 2021.

Counselling needs to be rendered to unemployed people, or the risk of returning to crime to provide for their loved ones, increases, consequently the risk for going back to prison too.

With the unemployment level rising due to COVID, the economy will take a few years to stabilise, so entrepreneurship is strongly encouraged, however entrepreneurship must be accompanied by education in order for the small business to be legal and effective. There are many home based businesses that can be started for entrepreneurs, such as motivational speaker, covering books for school kids, tuck shop, mobile coffee bar, gardening, starting an NPO for community upliftment, shopping for the elderly, write a book, create and sell art, baking and facilitating courses. Should offenders become skilled, not only can they create employment for themselves, but possibly for some of their community members too.

On interviewing the ex-offenders, it was established through them that their views of future chances of success and actual success in re-entering the employment stream once released, is positively increased by Christian and secular education, especially with the high unemployment rate being one of their greatest challenges.

7.9 Kaleidoscope of art as education in prisons

There are many universal languages in the world, a means of communication that can touch the heart without saying an actual word, being: A smile, a wave, fashion, culture, emotion, maths, music, chocolate, dancing and art!

The prison constituency is one of the most excluded in society today. Expressive Christian art education supports individuals to fulfil rehabilitative intent, reduces violence within the prison system as well as reduces parolees' recidivism rates. Creative learning enables personal transformation, encourages spontaneous learning, and working with colours is therapeutic.

Historically the paradigm shift of the penal policy has reflected a wider social inclusion, concerning enhancing basic, key and cognitive skills. Art is costly. The challenges offenders face are having access to art supplies and not all prisons run art classes to teach offenders the skill.

(Matarasso and Chell: 1998, Jermyn: 2001) studies have shown that art benefits offenders in many ways, especially those struggling with self-worth, confidence and empowerment. (Langelid, Maki, Raundrup, Svensson: 2009) evaluated that art contributes to offenders improving their motivation, social skills, life skills and learning from mistakes. There is a resilient link between development of the right brain and art education and practise, which leads to higher thinking skills and emotional self-control (Stevens: 2000, Sautter: 1994, Feder and Feder: 1981). There is compelling evidence that the right brain associates with focused attention creativity, affecting patience, self-discipline and the ability to work in a team. (Blacker, Watson and Beech: 2008) advocate there is ample evidence to suggest that art provides a way to express and release destructive feelings such as anger, aggression and unforgiveness. Poetry, acting in a play, writing an essay or novel, painting, drawing, all fall into the bracket of 'arts' in the prison system. Those who pursued the arts, were more interested in improving their normal education levels and partaking in other vocational programs for self-development.

Conclusions drawn from the research suggest that Christian art programs as education for offenders in South Africa, helps them develop improved mental perspectives. Offender behaviour patterns and obedience to prison authorities improves and they find a voice, as a pictures they mirror the famous statements, 'Speaks volumes, or, speaks a thousand words.'[52]

7.10 Melody of Christian music as education in prisons

Jesus himself sang a song 'Hallel' a Jewish prayer and verbatim recitation from Psalm 118, just after the last

---

[52] https://onlinelibrary.wiley.com/doi/abs/ - The Rehabilitative Role of Arts Education in Prison: Accommodation or Enlightenment? – Downloaded April 2021.

supper and just before he reached the Garden of Gethsemane and Golgotha (*Matthew 26:30 and Mark 14: 26*).

'When we play music and sing in prison, we have a special time in which to express ourselves, to put away the façade of being tough and seeing violence and all the things that hurt other people. We don't have to be who we are not, we can feel and be what we really want to be. I am exposed to a world of classical and gospel music, which I have never had the privilege of knowing before. An incredible break from some of the horror around us.' ~ Quote Prisoner in face-to-face interview.

The multi-faceted nature of music can take people on unexpected journeys, one that offenders often do not expect. There are two interactions that evolve from music in prisons, the relationship between offender and tutor 'mentor,' and the transformation that takes place of the learner. The relationship between offender and tutor within the criminal justice system, is a vital element to increase the offender's confidence, ownership, sense of belonging, motivation and self-determination which slowly moves the offender away from his criminal identity, a process called desistance (McNeil: 2011). This transformation leads to trusting the offender to taking on new responsibilities within their institutional communities, a key element in the wider offender education and preparation for transition and integration back into their home community. The tutor plays a considerable role in inspiring this conversion.

The crucial factor of assembling meditation with music is not being detached from one another, but integral to each other. The dual process of shaping and being shaped through music cannot be separated either. Social music singing, acts as a catalyst for evidence, of positive behavioural and emotional change in offenders. These changes were observed by prison authorities, family members and fellow offenders. Listening to and internalising the music, assist the offenders with communication, working together and developing relationships, listening to others and upliftment of moods. Gospel music draws offenders closer to God, increasing the scale of their relationship with him which creates a yearning to know more, seek more and learn more.

Music is part of our everyday lives, we sing whenever we can. We sing to put a baby to sleep, to comfort someone, to show respect for a leader, but more importantly, we and gospel music were created for the purpose of worshipping God. There are various forms of worshipping God, but singing is one of the main ones. Music as a universal language, is a gift from God to all human beings. Music is influenced by different cultures and as missionaries travelled, they took the songs with them.

There is good and bad music in every culture and therefore, we need to rely on the Holy Spirit to show us which is the good and acceptable songs and music to sing and play to God. In church, we do not worship the pastor or choir or worship leaders, we worship God and the words of the songs we sing must make this point clear. God wants us not to worship him in words only, but in Spirit and in truth. This means singing in full faith to God who is listening, with our own spirits to God's Spirit and when we sing like this, it moves our hearts and God's heart. Music leaders need to lead people to sing like this. Do not neglect to sing The Lord's Prayer from time to time. The Lord's Prayer, while given indiscriminately to all Jesus' followers, has a special application to leaders. According to Luke, Jesus gave this exemplary prayer to his immediate followers, who became conscious of their need for schooling, in the spiritual art of praying, while observing their Master pray, as we read in (*Luke 11:1*).

In the Tabernacle singing was very important, men and women from gifted families were trained to lead the singing and play the instruments. Today, musicians and worship leaders must be born again believers. [53]

A song leader needs to be:

- Called by God
- Anointed by God

---

[53] Leading the worship should not be like a traffic officer at a busy corner, but instead like a man riding a horse, sometimes he holds the reigns tight and steers the horse in a certain direction and other times he gives the horse freedom to run where it wants to.

- Have a clean heart
- Be willing to learn and teach others
- Able to lead the congregation to understand that the music is there to assist them to worship God
- Able to assist people to offer their singing as a living sacrifice of praise to God
- Able to match the songs of the worship session to the theme of the sermon
- Able to be led in song by the Holy Spirit
- Able to mix the music to suit old and young alike

God speaks during worship services and people say, 'When the praises go up, the blessings come down.' Singing moves the Holy Spirit, many prophetic words are spoken during worship services. Singing is where heaven and earth meet. If the worship in the church feels 'dead' people do not experience spiritual growth.

Writing new songs to sing in church is wonderful and everyone has the ability to learn a new song or write one. By taking a few bible verses, a psalm, or a poem and following a few guidelines, they can compose a song in eight easy steps:

- **Pray**: ask God to help you compose a song
- **Theme:** think about the needs of the people
- **Bible teaching|** choose a relevant bible verse
- **Chorus:** find words that are meaningful sung over and over again

- **Tune:** let a tune enter your head that suits the words, using a musical instrument
- **Verses:** write some sentences where the last words rhyme
- **Check:** easy rhythm, sing in your own language, main message of the bible verse
- **Record:** sing and record it, play it to your friends and ask them to help you improve on it

Music, singing and dancing:

Many churches do not allow dancing, but many African churches whole congregations love dancing, depending on the cultures represented in the congregation.

The dancing should be to honour the Lord, joyful and respectful. In (*2 Samuel 6: 5*) King David and all the Israelites danced for the Lord, in a joyful manner. Singing and dancing during services makes it special, but the dancing should not focus the attention on the dancer, but on the Lord himself.

Chapter 8   THE ABYSS OF PEDOPHILIA AND NECROPHILIA

8.1 The effects of sexual sin, for adults and children.

Sexual abuse is a controversial issue, worldwide. Its prevalence cross all boundaries of gender, race, culture, age, class and religion and reports on it are rapidly rising. Rape, incest, pedophilia, necrophilia, inappropriate touching, sodomising, incest, bondage and torture, flashing, sexual harassment, forced to watch pornography, trafficking – and many of these listed are accompanied by kidnapping, victimising, abuse, murder and death. There is also contact sexual abuse, non-contact sexual abuse and sexual exploitation – where the perpetrator gains financially by the abuse, such as prostitution or pornographic materials being sold.[54]

If children are relatives of the paedophile, sexual abuse takes the form of incest. Victims of pedophilia tend to be young children, who are beginning to mature physically (Rice and Harris: 2002). Child molesters rationalize their sexual behaviour as 'loving the child' not abusing them. They never consider the suffering psychological effect they have on their victims. Every victim experiences sexual trauma in a different manner and to a different degree.

---

[54] Religion and social development, Chapter 7, Part 2, Page 108.

Whether the abuser is known or unknown to the victim, the effects are devastating and for some the encounter happens once in their lifetimes, for others the abuse continues for years and most times, by a trusted adult family member or friend, Many sexual crimes do not get reported and the perpetrators are known to the victim, such as first dates, blind dates, casual dates or romantic acquaintances. When the child-victims eventually grow up they finally understand that they were powerless to protect themselves and not responsible for what happened, even though they may have felt guilt from childhood into adulthood.

Sexual abusers cannot be categorized, they often seem to be pleasant normal people, the friendly neighbour, that person that helps you with your flat wheel along the side of the road, the truck driver giving you a ride to the next town, the friendly clown at the children's party, the janitor that fixes everyone's plumbing and worst of all sometimes Christians in leadership positions including the pastoral level. It is believed that many abusers have experienced abuse themselves. Their thrill is having control, power and authority over the victim.

Sexual abuse victims obtain a very low self-esteem and have learned to see themselves through distorted lenses.

This unfortunately forms their identity as they adopt the message that was carried over to them by their abuser – 'You are worthless, unimportant, no one cares about you, no one will miss you and you are only good for one thing.' Unfortunately, we do not always see things the way they are, they see things the way we are or think we are. Girls who were sexually molested by their own fathers, grandfathers or step-fathers, have a distinct distorted vision of God the Father, which needs to be restored. They blame themselves and think they must have done something to deserve it or provoke it, which leads to feelings of self-hate, shame and guilt.

There are 2 basic emotions and all other emotions stem from these two: Love and Fear. Fear promotes guilt and shame, two emotions that Satan feeds on, causing the victim to feel dirty, spiritually unclean, undignified, depressed, oppressed and impure. They may inflict self-harm, have poor social interaction, intensive attention seeking, running away from home or resort to attempting to or actually committing suicide. They also believe no one will ever love them, which can rob the victim of their joy and God's plan for their life.

These victims also struggle to build normal loving relationships and may experience problems with normal sexual intercourse. Women particularly, in this case will wear baggy clothes to hide their beauty or develop eating disorders. They usually excel at school or cannot cope with school work at all.

They could develop an obsession with sexual activities, increased masturbation, molesting other children, promiscuity and unwanted pregnancies. Early exposure to sexual activity affects a woman's physical development and perversely abdicates the objective of blossoming into womanhood beautifully and naturally. They also question God's role in their lives and why he 'allowed' these things to happen to them. They could direct their anger at God and possibly never want to set foot in a church, especially if the perpetrator or abuser was a church going member.

Stockholm syndrome (SS)

SS is a psychological response which occurs when abuse victims or hostages bond with their abusers. This connection takes place over days, weeks, months or years during the captivity period. SS victims often develop post-traumatic stress, nightmares, insomnia, flashbacks, confusion, are easily startled and have difficulty trusting others. With this syndrome, victims tend to sympathise with their abusers. Over time, some victims develop positive feelings towards their abusers or captors, often helping them escape if the police are on their tail. The victim being brainwashed and lied to by the captor or abuser, may even develop negative feelings towards the police.

This does not however, occur with every victim and is a condition that psychologists or doctors describe as a coping mechanism which helps the victim manage with the trauma or terrifying situation. Due to threats or lies, the victims avoid retaliation or escape.

Victims of SS realise that as much as they hate the abuser, they need the abuser for survival. The abusers go to great lengths to convince the victims that only they 'the abuser' loves them and their families have forgotten about them, or believe them to be dead. The victims, once freed, have to be de=-programmed or re-conditioned from what they were taught by their abuser.

Sexual sin shows evidence of different demonic spirits at work in a person's life, such as: spirit of unforgiveness, orphan spirit, spirit of divorce, soul ties, spirit of lust and perversion, spirit of depression and fear, spirit of heaviness, spirit of suicide or death, spirit of infirmity, spirit of bondage and addiction, witchdoctors or Sangomas ancestry, lying spirit, spirit of jealousy, spirit of haughtiness, spirit of whoredoms and spirit of guilt. Deliverance and spiritual warfare are needed to set people free from these bondages.[55]

Silence about sexual abuse is not simply a manner of protecting someone, abuser or victim, it is a far more complex phenomenon. A number of these incidences

---

[55] Deliverance Workshop manual, Ps James Lottering, Warfare Ministries, Pages 19-23.

are sadly, never reported, so the victims suffer in silence. People with hidden hurt are usually very busy people, rebellious, lack a sense of belonging, a workaholic, or like to escape via watching movies all the time of playing games. One proven solution is forgiveness, which Author Philip Yancy described as an 'unnatural act,' which it is, because forgiveness is not an act, nor a feeling, but rather a personal choice to set oneself free.

Soul Ties

Soul ties is a spiritual connection between two people that have shared sexual experiences. The more sexual partners they have encountered, the more the web of soul ties binds them. Every rape and sexual incident, connects people with soul ties. Soul ties need to be broken, especially for someone who was raped or sexually abused, or had sexual encounters with partners outside of wedlock.

Genetic Sexual Attraction (GSA)

There is a condition called Genetic Sexual Attraction (GSA) which is a strong sexual attraction that develops between close blood relative family members, such as brother and sister, father and daughter, mother and son, first cousins, uncle and niece are some examples, which is particularly prominent in Mormon cults, but also more common than made known, in other citizens of society. However there are laws against it, as well as God's laws against it, as children born from incestuous relationships, often have genetic birth defects. In (*Leviticus 18: 6-18 and Leviticus 20: 11-21*) God prohibits such relationships. God designed love between family members in a healthy relationship environment, incest is something the devil introduced to distort love, diverting the truth of love as God designed it.

Demonic influence does not always mean one is demon possessed, as underlying 'anxiety' or demonic oppression, could be behind obsessions and compulsions.[56]

One of the most profound effects of child sexual abuse is the damaging impact it can have on the ability to form and maintain close, loving relationships, both intimate and platonic. It can affect the relationships that victims and survivors have at the time of the sexual abuse and for the rest of their lives. They may find it difficult to talk to partners, family and friends about the sexual abuse, preventing others from being able to help and offer support. Victims and survivors of child sexual abuse manage and respond to abuse in different ways, and their response can change over time.

For some, the psychological and emotional harm can be severe and at other times more enduring than the physical injuries sustained during the sexual abuse. Around the time of sexual abuse, children can experience a range of emotions, including fear, sadness, anger, guilt, self-blame and confusion.

---

[56] Introduction to Psychology and Counselling, Christian Perspectives and Applications, book by Paul D. Meier, Frank B. Minirth, Frank B. Wichern and Donald E. Ratcliff (Published by Baker Books) © Second Edition 2000, Pages 261.

Often child victims are rewarded for sex with the exchange of money, sweets or gifts for not breaking the silence of their abuse. Victims and survivors can feel humiliated or self-conscious, gain low self-esteem and will often not feel equipped or able to talk about what has happened. Repressed emotions are like fully blown balloons being held under water, they will keep resurfacing into adulthood, until properly dealt with.

To violate the body of a child is one of the worst deeds humans are capable of. It is particularly damaging when done repeatedly over a long period of time. Many adults still carry the deep scars of their trauma. There are a few factors to consider with the sexual abuse of a child- How old was the child when the abuse started? To what degree did the abuser have dominance over the child? Did the child always feel it was wrong, or start to feel sexually curious? How many years did the abuse continue for? Did the child ever try to tell anybody? Did the child in adulthood try therapy or counselling? Was the perpetrator ever caught and punished? Do their memories constantly haunt them? Have they been prayed over and broken the spiritual soul ties? Are the victims and perpetrators seeking help and functioning as normal adults, or is the abuse standing in the way constantly affecting them detrimentally?

When considering the effect child sexual abuse has on a victim and survivor's religion or spiritual beliefs, two particular themes have been highlighted. Victims and survivors start to question their religion and spiritual beliefs, particularly where the perpetrator was connected to their religion or faith, for instance a priest. They may also use religion and faith as a coping mechanism for resilience and recovery.

Research suggests that it can be common for victims and survivors to feel disillusioned with religion and spiritual beliefs after they have been sexually abused. They can feel abandoned or punished by God and begin to question their understanding of the world. This is particularly likely when the perpetrator is someone who represents God in the eyes of the victim, or has used religion or spiritual beliefs to justify the sexual abuse.

8.2 The Abyss of Pedophilia and Necrophilia's non-availability of Christian or secular programs.

a. Understanding pedophilia:

"Pedophilia isn't a crime. Child sexual abuse is the crime."
~ Quote Andrew Verrijdt, who is vehemently opposed to child sexual abuse and whose research is in progress at UCT's Department of Psychology.

In popular usage, the word *pedophilia* is often applied to any sexual interest in children or the act of child sexual abuse.

Although people who commit child sexual abuse are termed paedophiles, child sexual abuse offenders are not paedophiles unless they have a primary or exclusive sexual interest in prepubescent children. Some paedophiles do not molest children.

Studies have shown that only 8% of all paedophiles are females.[57] Some people believe that paedophiles are born that way, others believe they have a mental illness, or that perhaps they were molested as a child and others believe it's a choice they make to be the way they are.

If *pedophilia* is a mental disorder, why are we persecuting them and not trying to help them? It makes absolutely no sense.

Sexual orientation is defined as a lifelong attraction, which pedophilia is. Perhaps then, *pedophilia* is a mental illness and a sexual orientation combined? There are many paedophiles who do not act on their desires to have sex with children, but rather to view pornography of children but not harm them in person. There are child sexual abuse behaviours that include touching and non-touching. Sadly however, there are also those paedophiles who do tamper with children. When society observes a young man of 19, falling in love with and marrying a woman aged 59, their sexual orientation or preference is grimaced upon, but not seen as a criminal offence.

---

[57] Wikipedia.org/wiki/necrophilia – downloaded April 2021.

Paedophiles in their own minds, feel they deserve the same privacy and respect to have sex with whomever they want, just as everybody else does.

Practising paedophiles always manage to obtain employment working in places with children or near children, such as arranging children's parties, assisting at crèches, being a janitor at a school, being a security guard at children's schools,[58] etc. They also causally hang around outside school playgrounds and beaches where children are vulnerable. The sign of a paedophile is the teddy bear. Places where they molest children in groups, are sometimes disguised as guest houses, with a secret symbol of a teddy bear, or paedophiles walking on beaches will carry a bag with a teddy bear picture on, to advertise, notify and alert other paedophiles that they are welcomed in the area.

Many children have endured sexual abuse from a young age and only speak out in adulthood, causing traumatic inner emotional pain. Quite a few men in South Africa, have not only acted on their desire to rape a child, but to also kill them after the sexual deed, in order that the child will not recognise them and/or have them, convicted.

Pedophilia involves a cycle of deception in grooming the child, then sexually exploiting the child, then threatening the child if they ever tell anyone, then finally when the child reaches a certain age, they leave

---

[58] Case number A131/18 High Court Western Cape, assailant Cassiem Abrahams, Security Guard at school, raped an 11 year old girl, after three previous counts of rape and prison sentences.

the child and seek younger ones again, which gives rise to the traumatic Stockholm Syndrome (SS). As an adult, their authority enables the perpetrator to manipulate and coerce the child into submission and some form of compliance. Saving children from paedophiles is termed as 'saving little angels from big demons.'

There are four (4) categories that pedophilia falls under:

Infantophilia:	A paedophile that is attracted to babies 0 to 3 years old.
Pedophilia:	A paedophile that is sexually attracted to children aged 5 to 10 years old.
Hebephiliac:	A paedophile that is sexually attracted to children aged 11 to 16.
Paedo-Sadism:	A paedophile who is sexually stimulated by watching children being tortured[59] (Dark Web)[60]

Hebephiliac is currently the most active part of paedophile in the world today. An organisation that has researched pedophilia[61] believes that it may be easier to alter, than homosexuality.

---

[59] YouTube Clip Shaun Atwood and researcher of the Dark Web Ron Swanson, streamed 20 March 2021

[60] The darknet, a part of the internet that is partially hidden and only accessible via specialised software. Websites such as Hurt2theCore (H2TC), Hard Candy and 7axxn **via** Onion Router (Tor) needed to enter these websites, (Tor) was originally created to protect US government intelligence communication, or as a platform for whistle blowers

[61] The John Hopkins Clinic, in Berlin

Cognitive Behavioural Therapy (CBT) aims to reduce attitude, beliefs and behaviours that trigger sexual offences against children, which is not a short course, but a lifelong therapy, which is not Christian based. Most paedophiles do not come forward for assistance anyway, unless they are caught, for fear of judgement and persecution.

'If paedo-sadists exist, they're going to be found in the dark, underground web.'

~ Quote Andrew Verrijdt

One would only need access to the 'Dark Web' to see what filth and abuse is taking place against children. The Dark Web is a cesspool that fuels the most awful of minds. Oddly, preventative therapy such as victim testimonies, would have the opposite effect on a paedo-sadists, arousing them rather than steering them away from their actions. (Hazelwood, Dietz, Warren: 2009) cautioned investigators that a Sexual Sadist is cunning, calculating and accomplished at deception. He rationalises his feelings, feels no remorse or guilt and is in no way moved by compassion or sympathy.

Researcher of the Dark Web, Andrew Verrijdt, has excellent advice for parents: The best way to protect your child is to have the kind of relationship, where the child feels comfortable discussing sex and sexuality issues, added to this is the importance of comprehensive sexual education, a responsibility that should be shared by parents and the schooling system. An end needs to be put to treating sex as a taboo subject. Child sex offenders are afraid of the child that has an open, communicative relationship with someone they respect, because they are well aware that that is how they will get caught.

Another researcher of the Dark Web, Ron Swanson, reports that some paedophiles and necrophiles are attracted tortured children and animals. Most children abducted are homeless, or from troubled homes, the least likely to be missed. During these torture sessions, adult women sit on the heads of the children, stand on the children's ribs and rock to and fro, then dig their heel heels into the children's faces, pour boiling water over the children, cut a finger off, etc. The more the child is tortured, the more pleasure is experienced by the Sadist Paedophiles.

The adult torturers also skin cats, dogs or rabbits and nail them to boards. The individuals that are paying to watch these videos, the numbers of them on the Dark Web are growing exponentially. The police are using most of their resources in USA to fight drug wars, as opposed to using these funds to rescue these children from paedophiles. This scenario virtually makes the world close their eyes to these activities, rather than admit that these things are actually happening.

Although prisons offer 'sexual offences' healing programs that encourage behavioural changes, they do not have Christian or other educational programs to specifically assist paedophiles.

Prisons administer three-monthly 'Cyproterone or Depo-Provera' injections to reduce the sexual desire of the paedophiles, however they have no mental stimulation via published programs or group therapy, to appropriately assist.

When considering the effect child sexual abuse has on a victim and survivor's religion or spiritual beliefs, two particular themes have been highlighted. Victims and survivors start to question their religion and spiritual beliefs, particularly where the perpetrator was connected to their religion or faith, for instance a priest. They may also use religion and faith as a coping mechanism for resilience and recovery. It can be common for victims and survivors to feel disillusioned with religion and spiritual beliefs after they have been sexually abused. They can feel abandoned or punished by God and begin to question their understanding of the world. This is particularly likely when the perpetrator is someone who represents God in the eyes of the victim, or has used religion or spiritual beliefs to justify the sexual abuse, a typical example would be famous cult leaders.

Paedophiles need help, not condemnation. Christian counselling and possibly deliverance is the answer to healing, to always point the victims back to God. Secular programs and counselling take so much longer for healing to take place and the victim never feels as whole and delivered and free, as they would with the perfect healing Jesus gives.

Everyone in the world is longing to be loved, which is why pornography and pedophilia are part of the largest industries in the world, they are a counterfeit love and intimacy, opposing God's true love and intimacy as he planned and willed it. Pornography gives a person a momentary feeling of being known and vulnerable and satisfied and good, without the fear of rejection, as in the past they have perhaps experienced that giving yourself to others, only ends in pain and brokenness.

In South Africa pedophilia carries a prison sentence of only ten (10) years, the longer sentence of life only comes into play, if murder was committed with it.

b. *Understanding necrophilia:*

Necrophilia is a sexual orientation or mental illness that causes people to conduct sexual acts, rape or abuse on a corpse. It was identified and named in 1850 by Belgian psychiatrist Joseph Guislain.

Although genetic basis has been proposed as the reason for necrophilia, there is no real empirical foundation for it. No gene has ever been identified, however this leaves room for future research.

Necrophilia is termed as an obsession with, or an unusual interest in, or sexual stimulation by corpses. Necrophiles choose occupations that put them in a position to come into contact with dead bodies, such as mortuaries where autopsies are conducted, burial groundsmen and funeral parlours, but not limited to and definitely not inclusive of all mentioned. There is a distinct smell attached to a corpse, which involves putrefaction, which most people find abhorrent. Smell and propagation of emotion play a pivotal role in necrophilia.

Necrophilia is also known as necrophilism, necrolagnia, necrocoitus, necrochlesis and thanatophilia.

There are various classes of people, committing this offence:

Class 1	Role players	People who get aroused when pretending their partner is dead during sexual activity
Class 2	Romantic necrophiliacs	Bereaved people who remain attached to their dead lover's body
Class 3	Necrophiliac fantasisers	Those who fantasise about necrophilia, but do not physically interact with dead bodies, includes violent sexual fantasies

Class 4	Tactile necrophiliacs	Those around by touching or stroking a corpse, without actually engaging in sexual intercourse
Class 5	Fetishistic necrophiliacs	Those who remove objects or body parts from a corpse for sexual fetish reasons, without actually engaging in sexual intercourse
Class 6	Necromutilomaniacs	Those who obtain pleasure from mutilating a corpse, while masturbating, without actually engaging in sexual intercourse
Class 7	Opportunistic necrophiliacs	Those who do not normally have an interest in necrophilia, but take advantage of the opportunity if it arises
Class 8	Regular necrophiliacs	Those who want to have intercourse with the dead
Class 9	Homocidal necrophiliacs	Necrosadists who murder someone, in

		order to have sex with them
Class 10	Exclusive necrophiliacs	Those who have exclusive interest in having sex with the dead and cannot perform at all, with a living sexual partner
Class 11	Necrophagia	Sexual stimulation in eating freshly deceased or decaying flesh of the corpse, includes cannibalism and vampirisms
Class 12	Necropedophilia	Sexual attraction to the corpses of children

The motive for necrophilia is having possession of an unresisting and more importantly, an unrejecting partner, but lesser reasons include unavailability of a living partner, fear of women, belief that sex with a living woman is sin, the need to feel total control, expression of polymorphous perverse sexual desires and the need to perform limitless sexual activity.

There is little known treatment for necrophilia, except to do as with paedophiles, inject them with anti-androgens. In prisons there are many sexual offences programs to assist offenders, but none educational of secular or Christian for necrophilia. Healing programs to assist Necrophiles are desperate needed not only in South Africa, but worldwide, to address these heinous crimes, as in USA necrophilia is legal except in four (4) states.[62] An example of this, is currently in Massachusetts it is illegal to have sex with an animal, but not with a corpse.[63]

Victim selection by serial sexual murderers is based upon three factors: vulnerability, availability, and desirability.[64] The dead themselves, have limited legal rights and excuse the pun - but among these rights is, 'The right to remain silent.' In South Africa necrophilia carries a prison sentence of only 2 years, since it is listed under common law, the longer sentence of life only comes into play if murder was committed with it. The justice system needs to impose sentences that send a stronger message to other offenders, that such crimes will not be tolerated in the country and that deters others from committing similar offences, as well as committing crimes in general.

From a cynical point of view, men look for sex objects and fall in love slowly, women look for success objects, but although women tend to be allured by signs of wealth, status and a man's physical features, fall in love much quicker. A case study of a married woman that travels, always took her husband's pillow case with her wherever she went.

---

[62] Slate.com downloaded March 2021.
[63] metro.co.uk/2015/09/14/having-sex-with-corpses-is-still-legal-in-several-american-states
[64] Morton and McNamara, © 2005

At the hotel she slept at, she would slip his pillowcase over the hotel's pillow and that way sleep easier by smelling her husband's scent next to her. The sight of her delights her husband and the scent of him, readies her for love. In both male and female, oxytocin fuels the loving feelings of sexual contact. Eye contact, sight of lips, warm affection, flirting, kissing and touching all contribute to oxytocin levels rising, as the chemical builds attraction and gratification. There is however no guarantee that even after sexual encounters, the same two people would care for each other the next morning. In necrophilia, this romantic process is completely bypassed, the necrophiles brain is fuelled by testosterone, sexual fantasy, lust, a sense of entitlement, the thrill of no-one ever finding out and total lack of emotional attachment and empathy (narcissism) – so the act of sex is deemed a totally unnatural process.[65]

Narcissism, evil and an unsubmitted will are connected, according to (Peck: 1988) and claims that on the opposite side of the coin, mentally healthy people submit to a higher power, be it God, truth or an ideal that counteracts their own desire. The conflict between guilt and will, guilt must go and will must win.[66]

---

[65] Social Intelligence, The New Science of Human Relationships, book by Daniel Coleman, Published by Hutchinson, London © 2006, Pages 63-68, 198-210.
[66] Heart of Man: It's a genius for good and evil, book by Peck, Quoting Erich Fromm © Pages 175-177.

Man's continued captivation with death, united with the intricacies behind their want for intimacy, means that classifying necrophilia will always remain an incomplete and difficult process. Trying to understand what others want out of the living, could possibly help us comprehend what others want out of the dead. Those who place value in specific necrophilia's acts, have learned to think about the deceased in a compound and unique manner, and is our task to unpack human behaviour to determine where these individuals have found corpses, to be preferable to the living.

Necrophiliacs need assistance, not condemnation, but where does the church stand in this assistance queue? Is anyone besides secular psychologists equipped to deal with counselling and ministering to them?

Marital rape by necrophiles

Some necrophiles are married and rape their wives, or strangle them for 'dead' role play, a serious and dangerous game. Does marital rape exist? Yes, marital rape is a criminal offence. Sexually abused wives have challenged the pastoral care praxis with their terrible pain, shame and degradation in their homes because of the way their husbands treat them sexually. These women bear their lot with such courage and they have made it known that ministers and counsellors are not doing enough to lighten their burden. This seeks to present the Christian community with well-researched evidence that women are crying out for liberation from the pain of marital rape.

Many women during their working day feel and think in their hearts, 'I wish this day could never end. Going home at night is a nightmare I have been praying to wake up from for the past abusive years of my marriage.'

There has been an observation that the church has a way of using scripture in therapy in a way that condones oppression. In the case of intimate violence, texts such as (*Ephesians 5:22*) Wives submit to your husbands as the Lord and (*1 Corinthian 11:3*) But I want you to understand Christ is supreme over every man, the husband is supreme over his wife and God is supreme over Christ are cited to the women during therapy to silence and put them under condemnation, when they cry out for help.

There is a curiously loud silence on the subject of sexual conduct or behaviour between husband and wife in an abusive marriage, as it is considered taboo to talk about it openly. There is something about the trauma of constant humiliation, which marital rape is, that causes the victims to lose sight of God. They struggle to reclaim human dignity. The church lacks a method of care that is used to ensure that the teachings given about sexual benefits are for both partners.

The bride is taught these words, 'You have to work harder at being a better wife, submit yourself to your husband, he is the head of you, as Christ is the head of the church, pray so that you can endure this pain and remember God will never give you more than you can bear, divorce is sin. Your husband rules over your body, not you.'

Sexual violence is a private torture. A person that has lust forgets that each person is special and three-dimensional with a body, soul and spirit. Sexism, just like lust, turns the woman into a piece of property and her thoughts on the matter are never considered. Sex, as God intended it to be, is important for both spouses and the husband should thrive to make sexual intercourse as pleasant as possible for his wife, so that they can both experience the joy what the Bible ascribes to, not as torture or duty.

Most women that experienced forced rape, declared that their husbands used their 'superior physical strength' to control them during intercourse. It was comparable to the idea of having had sex with a demon, not a man.

For some people, the church is a primary reference point in their lives. When faced with a personal crisis they turn first to their pastor. For them, the pastor can be a trusted and known resource and they may assume that the pastor will know what to do in this situation, because the experience raises basic spiritual questions for which the victim or offender needs counselling.

Some pastors may say, 'But they are married so how do you say a husband can rape his wife, it is his right to have intercourse with her because they are married.' In many cultures, it is believed that the husband owns his wife's body and can do with it whatever he wishes.

It would greatly enhance the ministry of pastoral care if the matter of caring for women as an oppressed group, because as long as sexual problems in marriage continue to be seen as private family matters, women will continue to be denied effective pastoral care. Christians in the church have been thus far not been able to effectively deal with this issue, thus turned a blind eye, which has aggravated the pain that the women live with. Breaking the silence counts!

The question raised is: *'How does one make the pastors more aware of this problem, to make them acquire wisdom to deal with it, in order to journey with these women to wholeness?'* Women are made in the image of God and are worthy to be treated with care, nurtured and loved by their husbands. Christian education is key to combating marital rape.

Marital Rape has been described as 'one of the most serious violations of a women's bodily integrity, let alone a child's - and yet it is a term that many people still have a problem comprehending, with some still describing it as a 'contradiction in terms.'

Body decomposition:

Generally speaking a body lasts longer if air is not factor, near the corpse. If buried in light, dry soil, decomposition is quick. If the soil is damp, or has heavy clay around it, it takes long to decompose.

The body can take anything from three weeks to fifteen years to go through decomposition depending on weather, submergence in water, temperature or climate, snow, humidity and presence of insects or maggots. Once a female blowfly lays her eggs on the corpse, it takes fifteen days for the eggs to hatch into a maggot, which shreds and rakes the decaying flesh with the two hooks in its mouth. The maggot can breathe while it eats, meaning it eats twenty-four hours a day and grows to ten times its original size within four days from 2mm to 2cm. The maggot then crawls away from the body, to a dark place where it is at less risk of being eaten by a scavenger bird and will burrow 15cm into the ground, where it becomes a pupa and ten days later, hatches into a fly. The fly will use the balloon like blood bubble on its head to hit the ground like a battering ram, until it is free. It shakes its wings free and almost immediately starts to mate. Maggots are able to devour 60% of a human body in under a week.[67]

This is where the expression comes from used by necrophiles, 'The sweet smell of decay!' as they are attracted to the putrid, overbearing smell, which

---

[67] Forensics, The Anatomy of Crime, book by Val McDermid, Pages 45, 51 -82.

sexually excites them. It is through this decomposition state of maggots, that an Entomologist solves murder cases and proves when a murdered person actually died.

Since a body can take up to fifteen years to decompose in certain conditions, necrophiles often return to dig up the same body over and over, to sexually gratify themselves. The five stages of deterioration: fresh (begins with skin slippage and hair loss), early decomposition, advanced decomposition, skeletisation and extreme decomposition. A corpse's hair and nails can still grow up to three months after death.

Some necrophiles have found to tie their crimes to history and religion:

'The grave is a fine and private place, but none, I think, do there embrace!'[68]

~ Quote Andrew Marvell.

Some necrophiles follow the 'Aghori' new age teachings, where they believe everything is in god and god is in everything, including things like vomit, death and decay. They believe that 'nothing is unholy,' including 'falling in love or being in a sexual relationship with a corpse.'

---

[68] 'To His Coy Mistress' play by Andrew Marvell: Selected Poetry and Prose. Ed. Robert Wilcher. (London: Methuen & Co. Ltd.): 1986.

They find death to be a thing of beauty and the feel and smell of the dead to be sexually arousing. They believe God would approve of their sexual orientation and attraction. They reason and justify their actions by using history, where some royal family member's from centuries ago, used to perform sexual acts on dead animals, that there is absolutely nothing wrong with it.

In Islam, the prophet Mohammed permitted necrophilia by having sexual relations with dead bodies, He permitted one of his devotees to have close contact with his daughter that perished.

It was also accepted that an unmarried lady's spirit would not discover harmony, thus a wedding service solemnised the Kachin of Myanmar for a virgin who had died, which infers intercourse with a dead body.[69] Currently India is observing a rise in necrophilia cases, but have no laws to manage or prohibit the wrongdoing.

Since theatre began in the 1580's, despite the pressures form science and religion the mysterious power of the corpse captured the imagination of 'necrophilia love stories' and was not easily extinguished.

---

[69] Upsana Borah, A conceptual study to Necrophilia, A Review Article, ISSN2157-7145, The Department of Forensic Science, 2020, Page 1 -2.

Susan Zimmerman accentuated the centrality of the corpse in these debates at theatrical plays, where the relationship between the living and the transfigured corpse was a fascinating emblem in contrast to Christian belief systems.

The corpse was absurdly generative, not dead. It depicted death as a necessary punishment from God in penance for sin and to die and decay is become purified and redeemed, in order to live forever in the hereafter, but while the corpses were in a state of decomposition they were trapped in 'Purgatory.' (Charnes: 49) recasts the rotten corpse as an agent of erotic passion, no longer a sign of 'accusation' but rather the 'object of his desire' stating, 'Your beauty was the cause of that effect.'

In 1937 Disney produced the fairy tale 'Snow White,' who lay a long time in death without rotting or decay and when Prince Charming arrived he kissed her, infusing new life into her. The dwarves did not bury her, because of her rosy cheeks, she still looked alive so they kept her on display. The prince does not profess his love for 'Snow White' but is rather struck by her beauty as he states, the 'beautiful female corpse.' The prince insisting that he can see her body at all times, even though she is dead, is not only fixated and disturbing, but points to his power and control over her, yet also shows that in her death she holds power over the man, as the prince fell into a trance like state, as she was 'so beautiful he could not take his eyes off her.'

Other movies that cast zombies and vampires, such as 'The Rise of the Dead' and 'Bernie's Weekend Off' also encourage necrophilia, albeit subtly.

In what is today considered pedophilia, incest, necrophilia has been intricately interwoven into fairy-tales and it is argued that the effect movies have on society are widespread. Movies with these motives lay the cultural groundwork for it and encourage fascination with dead bodies, incestuous relationships, pedophilia and other taboos, solidifying that men have power over women and the notion that 'good women' are submissive, pious, pure and best keep their mouths shut.[70]

Identifying the actual crime criteria:

'We should treat the dead with respect. In death, money doesn't matter, material possessions don't matter, but dignity is what we should care about.' ~ Quote by Gung Tresna,
Lifeguard at Kuta Beach following the terrorist attack in Bali, Indonesia.

Demonic influences, perhaps even family curses, play an integral role in pedophilia and necrophilia. Many Christians believe that if demons are cast out of these individuals, they will heal.

---

[70] 'The Sleeping Beauty in the Woods' Tales of Passed Times by Mother Goose with Morals, book by Charles Perrault, Trans. R. S. Gent (New York: J. Rivington, 1795), Pages 57-58.

However, man is a creature of habit and may after a time, return to it, as the mind proves to be the greatest battlefield.

When a sexual act alone, or with aggression simultaneously, is attached to a murder, the act is termed a 'lust killing,' the killer otherwise described as 'One who has made a vital connection between sexual gratification and violence (Holmes: 1991, Page 67).' When a killing is conducted to hide a sexual crime, or to eliminate a witness, it is termed 'Killing after sexual act to destroy evidence' (Bartholomew, Mite and Galabally: 1975) and is deemed a sexual killing.

Sadism, associated with sexual killing is thought to be the most prominent within the lust killing category, as well as necrophilia coupled with mutilation and cannibalism, however there is too much variation of manner and types of killing to properly distinguish such cases.

A disturbing fact is that many necrophiles have sex with the living and with the dead, although their preferred inclination is with the deceased. An example of this is that the perpetrator could have killed the victim in an anger rage, because the victim fought back, but the intent was only sadistic rape (Malmquist: 1996). In these cases, anger management treatments are considered more effective for offenders.

Since sex and killing are connected in so many different manners and for diverse reasons, nature of the motivation and nature of the sexual element needs further exploration to be properly established and identified. Necrophilia can similarly take place, without the act of killing.

Criteria that meets inclusion of these crimes, as follows:

- Offender disclosed sexually assaulting victim after killing them
- Evidence from pathologist of post mortem sexual acts/behaviour
- Offender disclosed post mortem sexual behaviour, often coupled with motivation
- Evidence of sex with unconscious or deceased victim
- Offender disclosed since conviction, sexually assaulting the victim after the act of killing

Because of the bizarre nature of these crimes, the general perception people have is that it is a rare occurrence, however these crimes are more common than we think and unfortunately are never reported, so go undetected, unless the perpetrator is careless and forgets to put the corpse back in the fridge.[71]

---

[71] Dr Henry Lerm, Lawyer with the South Africa Legal Aid Board.

It seems imperative that as more crimes conducted by paedophiles and necrophiles surface, the prisons need to include pedophilia and necrophilia in their sexual offences healing programs, not only anger management, until such time as fully determined if these offenders should be placed in prisons, or institutions for the mentally ill.

Grief experienced by the loved ones of the victims:[72]

Whether parents of a child who was raped or murdered by a paedophile and/or necrophile, or whether loved ones of deceased people who became victims of necrophilia in autopsy rooms, mortuaries or graveyards, the emotional pain reactions need therapeutic attention, via grief counselling. While specific factors affect the mourning process of a violent death for instance, friends and family members could turn to blaming themselves or each other or getting stuck in living in a 'bubble' of constantly asking themselves, 'What if…?'or 'If only I …' However, when this violence is coupled with pedophilia or necrophilia, especially if conducted by someone they all trusted, how do they process and cope with it?

The added suffering of this knowledge and revelation, disturbs the emotional equilibrium and often causes loved ones to function abnormally, living in a state of shock and perhaps never getting over it,

---

[72] Grief Counselling and Grief Therapy, book by Author J. William Worden, Published by Routledge, London, UK © Third Edition 2001, Pages 88-89, 125-128.

causing complicated grief reactions. The death of a child has an impact on whole communities. Some families and friends manage to cope with the grief, through establishing a trust fund in the child's name and running awareness campaigns, as a way of the child never being forgotten or to add meaning to the life they lived (Brice: 1991). Some run therapy groups helping others to overcome their grief too, though organisations such as Compassionate Friends where empathetic talking and listening is available to family members that are grieving. Some never talk about their grief, ignoring the lives of the other siblings and building shrines for the one child that died and the living siblings are thought of as too young to understand what has happened, so grief counselling is not sought.

The experiences and reactions of the bereaved parents, is pivotal to the loss of a child and the impact it has on the family. Parents build the bonds of social and historical dimensions in a child's life (Klass and Marwitt: 1998).

Many couples lose touch with sexual intimacy, driving the parents further away from each other and driving the divorce rate higher. The shared loss creates a profound bond between the parents, yet the loss creates estrangement in the relationship.

Some loved ones forgive and some never forgive, hating the perpetrator and live angry and bitter and feeling cheated, with guilt feelings or constantly find someone to blame. Untimely deaths of children, are harder to deal with that anticipatory grief and leaves parents with many regrets, triggering suicidal notions, blaming God and an increased need 'to understand why.'

Parents should be given the option of whether to see the child's corpse or not, however not encouraged if the child was mutilated. This applies to loved ones of necrophilia victims too.

Pathological and unresolved grief, complicated grief, delayed or unexpected grief raise abnormal grief reactions that intensify the loved ones to feel overwhelmed, resort to maladaptive behaviour patterns, become either aggressive or passive, lose their passion for life, or remain in a state of grief without progression after the mourning process nears towards healing (Horowitz: 1980).[73]

Dealing with grief, when a narcissist feels no remorse, provokes anger and hate to levels that can provoke a person to murder for revenge and unless forgiveness takes place and depending on God, on the part of the loved ones left behind, they will never progress to true healing.

---

[73] Grief Counselling and Grief Therapy, book by Author J. William Worden, Published by Routledge, London, UK © Third Edition 2001, Pages 149-159.

There is a danger in belonging to a support group for years and years and not progressing to healing.

Statistics in a study conducted in HMP England:[74]

Her Majesty Prison in England conducted a survey on sexual crimes, coupled with murder, paedophile and necrophile related crimes. From the 100 prisoners interviewed, the ages ranged from 16 to 50 years old, 55 of them raped and killed strangers and the remaining 45, raped and killed someone they knew. 3 of them were convicted of multiple killings, while 97 were convicted of single killings. Information was collected on the progress of those who attended a Sex Offender Treatment Program (SOTP), where a battery of psychometric measures are administered before and after treatment.

During the running of the program, several additional potential treatments needed emerged (Harris and Hanson: 2000). A significant total of 81% of serial and single killer sex offenders were addicted to pornography and 37% of these were sadists who were sexually stimulated by strangling, causing harm or pain, humiliation and violence, instilling fear on their victims. These sadist offenders prefer a living victim, whom they kill themselves, then sexually abuse or mutilate the corpse. Strangulation made up 61% of the deaths related to these sexual crimes.

---

[74] Sexual Homicide and Paraphilia's: The Correctional service of Canada's Experts Forum 2007. Downloaded April 2021.

(Brittain: 1970) defined that sadistic paraphilia killers often had a history of cross dressing and voyeurism (nosiness) and show signs of having keen interest in indecent exposure, peeping, obscene phone calls, mystic coded letters and fetishes. They are also found to be very lonely and feel misunderstood.

Of the 100 offenders interviewed, 35 were child molesters who had not yet killed, but fantasised about it, while 17 child molesters had killed and sexually abused the corpse. 41% attacked their victim with sexual intention as opposed to 22% who found pleasure in cutting or incision wounding.

Of the paedophiles, 25% were found to be married men with children, while 20% were living alone and 55% were single or living in partnerships at the time of their sexual offence crimes being committed. Of the necrophiles, 9% were found to be married, 65% unmarried and 26% were single or living in partnerships at the time of their sexual offence crimes being committed.

18% had a history of grievances, hostility, anger and even hatred towards women, which they bottled up until they were able to kill. (Brittain: 1970) painted a picture of a rather pitiable individual, distinct and remote, insecure and regards himself inferior, including sexually inferior compared to other men and does not relate to people well, termed as 'social isolation or social outcasts.'

(Blanchard: 1995) found these sexual killers to be 'sex addicts.' (Tardif, Daaylva and Nicole: 2007) found one necrophile in the group was ridiculed by a prostitute, he proceeded to kill her and could only penetrate her after death, as she lowered his self-esteem. He remedied that by his power and dominance over her in her killing and after her death, humiliation.

Only 5% expressed feelings of guilt towards their victims, while the others conveyed no remorse nor expressed concern. 95% had narcissistic features or disorders such as entitlement, as well as a lack emotional intimacy. Both (Marshall and Hucker: 2006 and Tardif: 2007) concluded that major educational treatments for sadists, necrophiles and paedophiles will increase the extent to which they see their victims and other people as fellow human beings. Lack of concern is a credibly theorized need for programs to be put in place, more research in this area needs to be explored.

Interestingly, 24% suffered head injury during childhood and in 14% evidence was shown that the injury had a lasting effect on damaging their brain.[75]

---

[75] Sexual Killers and Post Mortem Sexual Interference Offenders: Assessment, treatment and Risk Management. Downloaded April 2021.

If no Christian prison ministries or counsellors are equipped to deal with this and no Christian programs put in place to specifically assist paedophiles and necrophiles, who are often also victims as they find no help nor have finances to pay secular psychologists, how will recidivism be reduced and how will rehabilitation be introduced?

The bible puts it best when Jesus speaks about the Great Commission, 'Whom shall I send?'

8.3 Missing children

Child abduction and trafficking, result in a high number of missing children annually in South Africa, 22,070 recorded child sexual abuse cases between April 2019 and April 2020. Over and above this 943 children were murdered in that annual period.[76]

Paedophiles are masters of manipulation to lure children, by hitting them at their point of interest, such as the internet trap, social media are methods of entrapment for child abduction, child trafficking, child sex pornography and other forms of sexual assault or abuse. Paedophiles will pose as a child to attract a child, they will use fake images and fake internet or dating profiles, text messages of what the vulnerable child 'needs to hear,' to convince the child they are old enough to make their own decisions and convince the

---

[76] Eye Witness News Crime Statistics, April 2020 – downloaded April 2021.

child not to tell their parents, as well as convince the child that their parents don't care about them, promise the child a modelling career or fame or money. They lure the child to meet them on a street corner, or a mall, etc. and end up kidnapping the child for trafficking, drugging, prostituting and sexually abusing them. Very early in the abduction the child gets threatened that they will kill their entire family if they try to escape, or that their parents don't love them or want them back anymore.

It is so important for parents to monitor children on their computers, social media, control their website usage and make use of age restriction limits, as well as awareness of children giving out their personal information.

Aggressive pornographers are using the following new strategies in marketing and technology to push pornography to users:

Porn Napping	The purchasing of experienced domain names, then redirect the users to their own sites
Cyber Squatting	Buy legal domain names and place explicit pornography on the site
Doorway Scams	Pornographers have figured out how to use search engines to get their website names high on the search engine, so it pops up when someone is searching for perfectly legitimate information, but lured to click elsewhere
Misspelling	Pornographers may take domain names of legitimate sites and use common misspellings to get the user to use their websites
Advertising	Create fake system-error messages and as soon as clicked on, opens a porn site link, linked to the pornographer
Entrapment	If anyone falls prey to any of the above scams, a whole host of problems can be incurred[77]

---

[77] Ropalato, TopTenReviews.com/tricks-pornographers-play.html

An organisation called the Pink Ladies warns about the dangers parents must look out for, to prevent their children from going missing. There is nothing worse for a parent, than not knowing where their child disappeared to. For years, tormenting thoughts and questions will occupy their minds: Who they are with, are they fed and safe and clean, are they alive or dead? Are they being tortured or sexually abused? Are they calling for me and I cannot help them? Are they locked up in a room somewhere, unable to escape?

According to the South African Police Service Missing Persons Bureau, one child goes missing every five hours in South Africa, which totals 1 825 annually, however only 77% of them are found.[78]

In an interview on True Crime South Africa, YouTube Podcast, dated 27 March 2021, A Social Worker, Zibeth Hansen at Brandvlei Correctional Centre in Worcester, stated, 'Rehabilitating and counselling paedophiles in the correctional services system, takes much longer than it takes with other prisoners, as there is a lot of shame and embarrassment attached to it for them. They find it difficult and are reluctant to talk, as well as very embarrassed, to ask for help.' The host Nicole Engelbrecht responded by stating that it is important for members of the public, neighbours, to listen to, assist and believe the child, who may tell them that they are being sexually abused.

---

[78] Missing Persons South Africa, website missingchildren.org.za – statistic information downloaded April 2021.

Child cultic abuse and trauma:

The victims once freed, have to be de-programmed or de-conditioned, from what they were taught in the cult, to believe they will not be killed. Polygamists for instance, although banished, still feel a bond with their abusive captors, due to the family members that remain behind in the compound.

Satanists fear for their lives and have quite a spiritual battle ahead of them, to recondition their minds to follow Jesus, a loving and non-punishable God who accepts them for who they are. Past rituals performed are difficult to erase from their memories, especially when guilt is coupled with the crime. Children brought up in satanic covens with Satanist parents, suffer sexual abuse and exploitation and often witness human sacrifices. Spiritual warfare is imperative to free ex-Satanists and children that have experienced such atrocities.

8.4 Personality type theories, criminal and personality profiling

There are several methods and lifestyle social practices of identifying necrophile and paedophile offenders, which determines the personality traits, characteristics and behavioural patterns of the offender.

Obsessive Compulsive Disorder (OCD) consists of two components, one of which is cognitive and the other behavioural, although the two do not always go together. Cognitive is directed at obsessions which consists of repetitive and unwelcome images, thoughts and impulses that invade consciousness, which are difficult to lay off or control. Behavioural is directed at repetitive compulsions which are behavioural responses to reduce anxiety associated with the compulsive thoughts (Clark and O'Connor: 2005). Once the compulsion was acted upon, the anxiety drained away.[79]

There are different types of criminal profiling:

- Geographical
- Historical
- Criminal Investigative
- Crime Action
- Investigative Psychology
- Behavioural Investigative
- Sociopsychological

The following items contribute towards a personality types of criminal profiling:

- Identity, race, ethnicity, gender
- Thought patterns
- Habits, modus operandi

---

[79] Psychology, The Science of Mind and Behaviour, book by Michael Passer, Ronald Smith, Nigel Holt, Andy Bremmer, Ed Sutherland and Michael Vliek, (Published by McGraw-Hill Education, UK) © 2009, Page 789.

- Uniqueness
- Instincts
- Ego, super ego[80]
- Behavioural patterns
- Regression
- Mentors, friends
- Personal signature clues left at crime scenes, to tease law enforcement officers
- Copycat traits of previous criminals, crimes
- Distinct victim targets
- Background, upbringing
- Historical trauma, abuse
- Lack of fatherhood
- Overbearing mother
- Teacher abuse, bullying at school
- Step parents influence
- Economic class background
- Lack of love and attention growing up
- Adoption, sibling separation, foster homes
- School records and behaviour patterns
- Criminal history, prison sentences, cases opened and dropped
- Religious background and beliefs
- Messy crime scene versus clean crime scene
- Corpse left intact versus dismembered, scattered corpses
- Propelling forces, triggers
- Committing crimes as a loners, with a partner or part of a group

---

[80] Theories of Personality, book by Duane P. Schultz, 10th Edition, Page51-52.

- Motivation, detrimental influences such as drugs, gangs, alcohol, peer pressure, money, sex, revenge, anxiety, bipolar, dark web, pornographic websites, wrong friends
- Love of torture, blood, cannibalism
- Warped sense of 'love' for corpses
- Distorted sense of 'love' for children
- Love for instilling fear into victims
- Love for grooming and manipulating victims
- A paedophiles will often assist the police and community to look for the dead body of the child that they themselves, raped and killed
- Violence, lashing out
- Torture of animals
- Deep seeded anger

A criminal leaves his personality traits behind at a crime scene, through his actions. His behaviour pattern shows his unique character traits, which are also identifiable to any sub-group to which he belongs.[81] According to Spiritual Care Worker at Brandvlei Maximum Security Prison in the Western Cape, Cape Town, 'Christian education does definitely alter the negative thinking and behavioural patterns of offenders, I have seen it happen before my own eyes, even paedophiles and necrophiles, and we have many right here in this prison.

---

[81] Criminal Shadows: Inside the mind a/the serial killer, Book by David Canter, © 1994 Page 12.

Some have sentences of up to 150 years, but our aim is still to help them, because God still loves them.'[82]

Criminal profiling assists the police, in how they approach the criminals, when closing in on them.[83] Much like predicting the weather, although rain predicted, it may not rain, but everyone will continue to look at weather predictions daily. Although criminal profiling is an integral part of police work, it has never proven to be accurate every time, yet still used worldwide.

Pedophilia is generally described as the rape or molestation of children by adults, from as young as a few months old babies to teenagers under sixteen. Many of these children have been kidnapped and sold into slavery. In the Catholic Church approximately 10% of priests are rapists of nuns or paedophiles of the orphans living in the nunneries, which has always enjoyed a major cover-up or denial status.

The Pizzagate, rooted in the discovery of a Romanian taxi-driver, who emailed John Podesta many times, giving clear reference to pedophilia in all its forms, from art to swimming parties, helped to expose pedophilia to a broad audience and Hillary Clinton and Dennis Hastert's names were at the top of the scandal's list.

---

[82] Face to face interview, Spiritual Care Worker, Brandvlei Maximum Prison, on 9 April 2021.

[83] An Appraisal of Forensic Science Evidence in Criminal Proceedings, Book by Norbert Ebisike © 2001 Pages 44 - 49.

Notwithstanding the British millionaire socialite Ghislaine Maxwell who on five of the six charges of grooming young girls, some as young as 14 years old, that she performed sexual acts on as well as coaxed to perform sexual acts on Billionaire Businessman Jeffrey Epstein. Epstein committed suicide in his prison cell after his arrest (a conspiracy theory as some speculate he may have been murdered). Maxwell has tried four times to apply for bail, but as a flite risk and been denied. Maxwell faces up to 65 years in prison. In a little black book, Epstein recorded all the rich men that flew on his private jet 'The Lolita Express' and the FBI is busy investigating all the names of rich and famous people that visited the island.

Recently a famous French modelling agency owner Jean Luc Brunel, was arrested for being part of that sex-ring. Prince Andrew has been accused of partaking in these controversies, but denies any involvement despite many witnesses that have come forward. Big names were mentioned of rich moguls that were blackmailed by Epstein for large sums of money, after being secretly filmed in compromising positions, with underage girls on James Island in the Caribbean that was owned by Epstein, a place the girls were trapped in and had no escape. Epstein would molest these girls under the auspices of 'massages.' Associated with Jeffrey Epstein and Ghislaine Maxwell, Prince Andrew, Queen Elizabeth's second son has also been accused by Mrs Virginia Giuffre of sexual abuse on three separate occasions by the prince, when she was merely 17 years old.

In a separate incident, Peter Nygard, a billionaire fashion icon to the world, dangled the promise of being a famous model and earning a lot of money, to lure young underage girls from 14 years old, to perform sexual acts on his business friends. He has had numerous adulterous affairs and forces any woman who falls pregnant from him to abort their babies, the foetuses are then used in labs to experiment on how he can perhaps live forever or stay youthful and not age. He has also been accused of having a blood transfusion from a child, with adrenalized blood, where the child was frightened and tortured before they were killed. Nygard is currently in prison at the age of 74 and his money nor fame can help him to get out. He is facing life imprisonment and denies all charges. Many young models went missing that were under his wing.

The list of names goes on, too many to mention in detail, but can be researched on the internet and YouTube.

These people are not going to stay in prison with long sentences and not reveal who the other people are that are involved, US politicians, judges and celebrities and when that bubble bursts, Maxwell, Nygard and Brunel may face the same fate Epstein did – suicide or murder – to keep the information of their pedophilia actions that they have hidden.

Information that is not properly disclosed to the public is that one million children in the USA go missing annually and that beyond pedophilia, satanic rituals are performed on them, including sodomy, torture, rape, murder, bone marrow and organ harvesting, and drinking of their blood.[84] Money plays a large role in perpetrators believing they will get away with murder or crimes of heinous nature and these crimes are not defined by people living in poverty stricken areas, or certain age or ethnic groups, etc. as we can see it happens among the rich and famous too.

Various perplexing personality problems that reveal themselves in adult life, are deeply rooted from impressions we experienced in the womb. These memory traces, often referred to as 'pre-memory impressions,' influence our most fundamental emotional responses, thought processes and behavioural patterns. What happens in the womb, establishes the foundations of our life. The types of impressions made on our lives in the womb stage, include 'I have a right to live, I do not have a right to live, I am wanted, I am rejected, I am accepted and belong, I am not accepted and will be given away.' Thus challenges adults face, based on the womb experiences could be anxiety, depression, autistic, or never feeling like you belong. Paedophiles prey on vulnerable children that are neglected or rejected by parents.

---

[84] Paedophilia, Empire Satan, Sodomy and the Deep State, book by Joachim Hagopian, Foreword by Robert David Steele, © Published by Amazon Pages 4-7.

These adult behaviours manifest in these ways:

- Existence issues, thoughts of suicide, struggle with life and death.
- Rejection issues, feel worthless, not good enough to be loved, accepted or cared for.
- Anxiety issues, panic attacks, restlessness, uneasiness, suspicion.
- Autistic disorders, unable to maintain close relationships.
- Insecurity, affects stability and tussles with a sense of belonging, which causes uncertainty, lack of confidence.

'One cannot give to the world, what you have not received from childhood. When God restores you, he does not restore you to your original condition, but rather to His original intention for your life.'[85]

Five main theories of personality types:

Phlegmatic	Emotionless
Choleric	Active, irritable
Sanguine	Happy
Melancholic	Depressive
Repressive	True personality hidden

Personality is the ingrained pattern of thoughts, feelings and behaviour which remain consistent across time and through different situations. People tend to

---

[85] In person interview, Ulrich Lottering, Managing Director NFCSA, on 5 April 2021.

act differently, based on who they are talking to or interacting with. These patterns manifest based on prior contingencies, such as reinforcements, punishments and conditioned responses. Behaviourism will explain sinful behaviour, but not the reason why people sin. Defence mechanisms protect individuals, to protect from painful experiences and emotions.

Repression bars or banishes memories, feelings and perceptions that would arouse discomfort from childhood, such as being sexually molested. Many people who were sexually molested by paedophiles as a child, will express that they 'simply went far away to another place, in their minds' while the sexual deed was being performed on them, as a protective coping mechanism. As people grow in Christian maturity, forgiveness takes place, conflicts are resolved and repression walls come down. A chief source of emotional pain, is lack of intimacy with God.[86]

Pain in one's life will continue, while it remains hidden. Unless God intervenes and brings new life and his healing touch into these broken and wounded areas, these negative things will be passed from generation to generation. Satan's strategy is to hold whole families captive through generational curses. The good news is that the devil has no power without permission, so if your grandparents let him in to an open door through sin or disobedience, you have the right to kick him out, through the blood of Jesus and the Power of the Holy

---

[86] Introduction to Psychology and Counselling, Christian Perspectives and Applications, book by Paul D. Meier, Frank B. Minirth, Frank B. Wichern and Donald E. Ratcliff (Published by Baker Books) © Second Edition 2000, Pages 225-226, 240.

Spirit, that can set us free from these bondages, as redemption rescues us from all these losses.

When running Christian education courses to assist different personality types, this grid of information will prove to be helpful:

Personality Type:	How Individual Acts:
Predator	Has the wrong motive 'hidden agenda'
Dominator	Has all the answers – tries to take over the class
Spiritualizer	Constantly preaches and talks 'Christianese' – to him every issue has a deep spiritual solution, answers 'Amen' to everything instead of 'Yes'
Chatter Box	Rambles on and never quite gets to the point
Justifier	Hopes the group will ease his conscience, has made bad choices in the past and has no interest in taking responsibility for it
Socialiser	Looking for a 'quick fix' to ease his loneliness – usually not teachable
Doom Advisor	Gives negative / bad advice during the class
Wall Flower	Shy person who needs to be drawn out to know he fits in. Hit him at his

	point of interest and see how he blooms
Mood Swinger	Bi-polar or chemically depressed – if medication was forgotten, will be disruptive and easily distracted
Despondent	Severe depression, negative, possibly suicidal and in need of prayer and professional help immediately, his negativity will affect the group
Joker	Joker of the pack, always disrupting the class with wise cracks, laughter and jokes. Sometimes humour keeps the class going, but depending on the topic of the day, to be monitored and managed. As facilitator/leader, remember that you are in control
Gangster	Usually disruptive, looking around to make eye contact with other gang members. Show each other secret hand signs, speak Sabela 'gang language.' Can be threatening and manipulative, by intimidating others in the class. They like to pretend they are paying attention, but their motives are selfish. Gangsters attend classes to see what they can get out of it or how they can benefit from the leaders – like food, phone money, needs

	supplied - but not because it can help them heal and grow!
Victim	Does not want healing. Their crisis draws the attention and sympathy they crave for and thrive on. Their identity is in their hurt. Everybody is at fault, except them
Enabler	Wants to take on and fix everyone in the group's problems

8.5 What is a stalking personality and how does it affect victims?

Most stalkers are men, however many women become stalkers, to ex-partners of past relationships. The average period of stalking duration is just over two, often terrifying years. Although difficult to believe, stalking often begins while the relationship is still intact and escalates after separation, which increases the risk of violence or murder.

There are different tactics of stalking:

- Technology or cyber stalking through social media, email or anonymous phone calls, social websites, chatrooms or WhatsApp groups, spyware, hidden cameras
- Strangers who have no reason whatsoever to record your personal information and be able to rattle off your telephone number or home address
- Physical stalking, being followed or spied on,

peeping Toms, letters in post-box, being waited for or watched

- Phone calls, blackmail, threats, unwanted gifts, messages, no respect of victim's privacy
- Physical and sexual harassment, assault, control
- Identity theft, financial harm, kidnapping for ransom, damage to victim's property
- Gets too close to the victim's children, using them as tools to have access, threaten or to instil fear in the victim
- Breaking in to the victim's house
- Fans who are obsessed with famous or public figures

There is a difference between intimate and non-intimate stalkers. Intimate means people you know, non-intimate means someone you do not know. Most stalkers reoffend even after receiving a court order, a definite red flag when they refuse to respond to court interventions. Some ways to recognise stalkers is how they create fear in their victims, manipulating them, crossing boundaries, not respecting the their victim's restrictions, physical or controlling abuse, personality disorders, low self-esteem, loners, living in a dream world of believing in their minds, 'One day we will be together,' or 'If I can't have him/her, no one else will.'

People who are being stalked, have high levels of distress, anxiety and fear. Reasons most stalking is not always recorded by the police is lack of evidence (recording of dates, times, events, venues), lack of witnesses, fear of the stalker, not a police but a private matter, consequences of calling police are dire, stalking not severe enough to be life threatening, belief that the police won't do anything or they will not be believed. Stalking is a complex crime and more research needs to be done to assist the frustrated victims, feeling helpless in their situation.

Children do not pay attention to their surroundings as much as adults do, so stalking would possibly go unnoticed and children are vulnerable and need to be protected at all costs.

8.6 The loophole of the 'insanity' defence

It is very possible for a necrophile or paedophile to legally avoid the consequences and paying the price for their crimes, by pleading insanity.

The loophole of insanity is an age old tried and tested method of literally getting away with murder and other heinous criminalities. The law of insanity is based on the assumption that when an insane person commits a crime in a fit of insanity, they do not have a guilty mind to understand what they are doing and that act is prohibited by law. Those found to be insane are neither morally nor legally guilty.

This defence includes two branches, *not guilty by reason of insanity* or *guilty but insane or mentally ill* which could result in either still going to prison, being committed to a mental institution or a psychiatric facility for an unspecified period.

Ways to judge criminal insanity is to determine if the crime was planned and committed with intent; and if the perpetrator was coherent and competent enough to understand the trail process and its outcomes (Borum and Fulero: 1999).[87]

Criminal insanity is a grey area which could have many twists and turns and surprising outcomes. There is however a difference between insanity and mental illness. Mentally ill persons who are incarcerated are a serious problem, as they do not receive the assistance they have a right to and need, for therapy and healing, which could lead to maltreatment and stigmatization (one of their rights being, the right to preserve their dignity).

Counting mentally ill patients into the ratio of recidivism, is prejudiced and unfair, however the widespread misconception is believed in many countries, that a mentally ill person is a danger to the public.[88]

The law recognises that under certain circumstances, some criminals are not responsible for their behaviour and it would be ineffective and perhaps unfair to punish them. In the case of homicidal necrophilia, prosecution would do well to frame questions in such a way that intent to kill is proven beyond doubt.

---

[87] Defiling the Dead: Necrophilia and the Law: Tyler C. Ochoa, 1997 – Downloaded April 2021.
[88] World Health Organisation – Downloaded April 2021.

Important factors in the evolution of the insanity defence

Factor	Year	Quotation
Daniel M'Naghten Rule	1843	It must be clearly proved that at the time of committing the crime, the accused party was labouring under defect of reason, from disease of the mind, as not to know the nature and quality of the act he was doing, of if he did not know it, that he did not know that what he was doing was wrong
Durham Rule	1954	An accused is not criminally responsible if his unlawful act was the product of mental disease or mental defect
American Law Institute	1962	1. A person is not responsible for criminal conduct if at the time of such conduct as a result of mental disease or defect he lacks substantial capacity either to appreciate the criminality of his conduct or to conform his conduct to the requirement of law

American Law Institute	1962	2. As used in the article, the term 'mental disease or defect' do not include an abnormality manifested only by repeated criminal or otherwise antisocial conduct
Diminished Capacity	1978	Evidence of abnormal mental condition would be admissible to affect the degree of crime for which an accused could be convicted. Specifically these offences requiring intent or knowledge could be reduced to lesser included offences requiring reckless or criminal neglect
Insanity Defence Reform Act	1984	A person charged with a criminal offence should be found not guilty by reason of insanity if it is shown that, as a result of mental disease or mental retardation, he was unable to appreciate the wrongfulness of his conduct at the time of his offence

8.7 The origins of evil, man's inhumanity to man.

Necrophile evils:

(Sheets-Johnstone: 2008:128f) states empathy and evil both have their roots in evolutionary heritage of humans, which stretch from biological and cultural backgrounds. What is evil, if not for violence, warfare, massacres, ethnic cleansings and male to male competition? (Veltesen: 1994: 84) augments that the nature of radical or unprecedented evil, the connection between deeds and motives and the relationship between thinking and judgement, as the 'banality of evil' is the blind commitment to doing one's duty, out of a human realm fundamentally characterised by a thoughtless diligence to duty and not from an emotional point of view.

The relative ease with which humans can close off social emotional feelings and succumb to decimating humans, is nothing less than shocking, cultivating brutality. The banality of evil flows not only from choosing not to do evil to others, but to use evil and brutality for personal advancement and chasing personal agendas.

Hatred promotes lack of empathy, therefore the blatant progression is clear, emotional failure which is lack of empathy, leads to cognitive failure which is lack of judgement, leads to evil.

Therefore, the question should no longer be, 'What/Who is evil?' but rather, 'What motivates evil?' (Sheets-Johnstone: 2008:128f) calls evil the 'heroic honing of males, for aggression and violence. Yet it is important to note that lack of empathy alone, does not constitute evil, just as a lack of judgement in itself, is not yet a motivation for evil, but only its potential.

From an evolutionary point, humans are born with a moral sense of right and wrong and have the capacity to perform good and evil. Prior to being able to rationalise actions and beliefs, the common criteria of rationality is that humans should act reasonably in the world and have reasonable beliefs about their actions. The revolutionary ethic's beginning point is the insight that morality (moral behaviour, moral awareness and moral codes), is the product of ethical behaviour. Some moral conducts are based on a drive to survive, others on a drive to destruction but more importantly God gave humans the freedom to make their own decisions.[89]

Erich Fromm, Author of *War within Man*, claimed that Adolf Hitler was a pure necrophilous type of personality, as 'he was fascinated by destruction and the smell of death was sweet to him.'

---

[89] Living Theology, Essays presented to Dirk J. Smit, Published by Bible Media 2013 © Pages 459 – 465 written by J. Wentzel and Huyssteen.

During the years of his 'success' during the war, it may have appeared that he only wished to destroy his enemies, the end of his days showed his deep satisfaction in witnessing not only the destruction of his enemies, but also of the German people around him and of himself. One soldier witness reported observing Hilter standing in a trance-like mode gazing at a decayed corpse and unwilling to walk away. Necrophiles dwell in the past and their feelings are sentimental. Characteristic of the necrophile is an attitude toward force, just as sexuality can create life, force can destroy it. For the necrophile there exists a polarity, that between those who have the power to kill and those who lack this power, the powerful versus the powerless. To understand men like Hitler and Stalin, lies in their unlimited capacity, willingness and power to kill, for which they are loved by necrophiles. Most people feared them, but necrophiles viewed them as heroes.

Closely related to necrophilia is sadism, all that is away from or directed against life, attracts them. A sadist wants to return to the darkness of the womb, his life is never certain, predictable or controllable. In order to make his life controllable, it must be transformed to death, as death is the only certainty for the necrophile. The necrophile can be recognised by his looks and gestures, he is cold, his skin looks dead and he often has an expression on his face as though he is smelling a pungent odour. (Hitler's face showed this expression).

A necrophile is orderly, obsessive and punctual.

They usually have an attraction to death and dirt and sadism. Any of these features may be more pronounced in one person, than in another.[90]

Paedophile evils:

Dr Fred Berlin, director of the John Hopkins Sex and Gender Clinic made a statement, 'People do not choose what arouses them- they discover it! No one grows up wanting to be a paedophile.'

One particular case stands out, which includes incest and gang rape, is a father named Alfred John who raped his own daughter of 13 years old, then held her down and 'calmed her and kept checking if she was 'OK' and that the 8 men from his paedophile ring, were not too rough or violent with her, during their gang rape performed on her.' *How ironically or iconically 'evil' is it, that this gang rape occurred on 31 October 2017, Halloween?* One of the 8 men in this paedophile ring was a former South African Christian Pastor, from Midrand, David Volmer. Her father, Alfred John got a sentence of 22 and a half years. The other 7 men received sentences that range between 3 and 13 years. This paedophile ring is known as the 'Evil 8.'[91] Her father, who was supposed to protect her, held her down for these eight other men to gang rape her, is the ultimate origin of evil and man's inhumanity to man example.

---

[90] War within Man, A Psychological Enquiry into the Roots of Destruction, book by Author Erich Fromm, Published by Cambridge, © 1963 Pages 10-23.
[91] Article by Joanna Menagh, Perth Australia, ABC Net News Channel, dated 31 October 2017, downloaded April 2021.

The pastor was found to have sexually abused her 12 times in the past, with her father's knowledge and permission and will be turfed out of Australia and deported back to South Africa, as soon as his sentence is up in 2027, or if granted early parole, in 2024. This girl child will have a deeply distorted view of God as Father.

David Volmer experienced crushing abuse from his own father, who was a drug and sex addict. David grew up surrounded by 'groupies of drug addicts' taking drugs at his house, with sex video's playing on the television all day long. He witnessed how his father physically and sexually abused his mother. In 2014 David sexually abused his first young girl victim, while his father watched with approval and satisfaction. When he was 16 years old, he was bullied at school and often wanted to commit suicide. This research proves that a family curse is filtered down to future generations through unconfessed sin, where a cycle of abuse continues, if not broken by the power of the Holy Spirit and the Blood of Christ Jesus.

As a husband and father of two children, David tried to hide his pedophilia from them, but was caught and exposed. He did not show remorse for the 13 year old girl that he abused, but did show sorrow for the wife and children he disappointed and deeply hurt.[92]

---

[92] The West Australia News Channel, Perth Now, Article written on 18 November 2017, by Kate Campbell, downloaded April 2021.

A paedophile who inflicts dreadful sexual abuse on a child, sees himself as the victim, but each paedophile's story and history is unique.

8.8 The consequences and impact of victim trauma

The trauma that victims experience, has a profound and devastating effect on not only the victim, but also on their loved ones. Crimes have varying and significant consequences through a number of factors. A history of trauma will have an increased trauma threshold, when a new crime is experienced. Although every victim is unique, they react to trauma and victimization in different ways and heal in different timeframes.

Everyone is affected by crime, either directly or indirectly, which increases fear. Crime has quite a financial impact on people, as insurance payments rise, the need for security gates, security guards, cameras, neighbourhood watches, first responders, fire fighters, hospitals, police, prisons, crisis centres, courts of law and other services. There is also survivor guilt to consider, when a group of people have experienced trauma and only one or two survive.

Most people are able to cope with the trauma of victimization, especially those attending counselling sessions, or are part of a support group. For others, they may turn to drugs or alcohol, attempt suicide, experience depression or be at risk of further victimization.

Emotions that surface from trauma include:

> If ***anger*** was a colour it would be bright red, as fiery hot as a volcano. If anger was a taste, it would taste like red chilies. If anger was a feeling it would feel like hot coals, an open flame or a turbulent pot of boiling water. If anger was a smell, it would be as awful as chicken compost laid on vast open fields on a hot summer day. If anger was a sound it would be as loud as a parent when you come home late for dinner.
>
> If ***joy*** was a colour it would be bright yellow, as happy as the sunshine. If joy was a taste, it would taste like ice cream, jelly and custard, streaked with hundreds and thousands of colourful dots. If joy was a feeling it would be a stream of happiness flowing through your body like an electric current, causing you to laugh and cry all at once. If joy was a smell, it would smell like the fragrance of a million softly crushed flowers flowing past you like a tantalising perfume. If joy was a sound, it would be like little children running and laughing and catching butterflies.
>
> If ***fear*** was a colour it would be black, dark and scary, not knowing what lurks in the shadows. If fear was a taste, it would taste like cardboard. You feel it, but don't really taste it. If fear was a feeling, it would feel like a huge ocean wave descending on you with speed, its crushing power making you feel helpless. If fear was a smell, it would smell like a building burning down with screaming voices inside, as you stand helpless and watch people die. If fear was a sound, it would sound

> like a thousand demons grabbing you and dragging you into a fiery furnace.
>
> If *love* was a colour, it would be a heavenly blue, as blue as the sky on a bright day in autumn or spring. If love was a taste, it would taste like a chocolate fountain, waiting for you to dip your tongue into it. If love was a feeling, it would feel like a moment in God's presence, which is much better than a thousand years anywhere else. If love was a smell, it would smell like the fragrance of fresh gentle rain on a crispy spring day. If love was a sound, it would sound like a shofar, the blowing of a horn, announcing the arrival of Jesus as He returns to fetch the bride He loves so much.
>
> God understands all of your emotions and how they make you feel. He knows when you are feeling up and when you are feeling down. He knows when you sit and when you stand, he sees and knows all.[93]

Every negative thought about oneself should be treated as contrary to what God thinks and says about you, as negativity is dangerous to your true identity and every negative connotation a trespassing from the enemy.

How can we assist trauma victims to heal?

Ways to assist people to heal from trauma include:

- Christian Support groups
- Christian Counselling
- Training workshops on victim empowerment

---

[93] Excerpt from The Only Way Out, Book written by Val Hamann, Published by Biblecor, Wellington © 2015, Page 31.

- Training and healing workshops for paedophiles
- Training and healing workshops for prisoners and ex-prisoners
- Healing workshops for victims of abuse and trauma
- Prayer partners
- God's word
- Education
- Find volunteers or mentors to spend quality time with the victims
- Create awareness
- Partner with government departments, police, NPO's or private organisations, who provide voluntary support services for general or specific traumas
- Establish more shelters
- Establish more aftercare centres and employment for ex-prisoners
- Engage and establish a relationship with local free medical services for victims
- Ensure victims have emergency numbers at hand in the event of further trauma or abuse
- Sensitivity training to health care workers
- Encourage more visits and care for their elderly family members
- Encourage victims in journaling

What can a victim of do to be free or healed?

- Turn to God and surrender the situation to Him completely, trusting Him for the best outcome
- Pray continually
- Sit it out without sarcasm or rebellion, talk the abuser out of it
- Victim to try and get on their abuser's good side
- Enlist the help of others, don't be isolated
- Fight back, but not in a way that will cause further harm or death as a result
- If abused in workplace by boss, walk away, resign from your job with a dignified and professional attitude
- Stay calm and focused and wait for an opportunity to escape
- Christian Counselling
- Find a Christian mentor

While support groups and counselling assist, only Jesus is the true healer!

It important that the victims and the counsellors accept that they will have conflicting views and need to meet each other half way, praying always for God's complete healing and deliverance in the victim's life. For some victims that escape, guilt is agonising, crushing and challenging, to overcome.

Abusers never tell their victims that they live in fear, but everything they do is driven by fear, remembering the abuse and torture of not complying with the abuser's demands.

The abusers in turn, fear their victims judging, hating, turning on them or exposing them. During counselling it may be possible that for the first time ever, the victim feels free to make a choice of their own, or have a choice to believe something that they are not coerced into.

Regardless of how and why the victim may have made hatred and bitterness their best friends, if they carry them around long enough they will feel eaten up alive from the inside out. They may possibly have spent their life, without releasing it or intentionally doing it, not focusing on emotional healing which is what their heart needs and instead, been focused on the punishment life has dished out to them.

8.9 The rationalization of pedophilia, child brides

Children born in poor communities are usually vulnerable to abuse. There are an average of 700 million[94] young girls all over the world between the ages of 5 to 15 years old, forced into child marriage with men much older than them, in the name of tradition, culture, customs and law, however this child bride status quo is veiled under the banner of *pedophilia.*

Most of these girls are raped into submission, during the so called *consummation* of the marriage, which occurs in urban and rural areas, with the child's parents and community leaders' consent.

---

[94] UNICEF

In poorer countries, the girls are sold to the men by the parents, as a means of obtaining money for survival and uplifting their economic status. The younger the girl, the more money they get.

In Bangladesh a staggering 71% of girls under the age of 18 are married, placing the country as one of the highest child marriage rate areas in the world. A simple piece of paper titled *Marriage Certificate*, makes it legal and right for the man marrying the child, but for the child who suffers the abuse, rape and early loss of childhood, loss of education and loss of a life of their human dignity, it is appalling. They rationalize pedophilia by way of socio-cultural and religious customs and economic consideration. The child victim is helpless. No legal complaints are filed and the abuser and community remain silent and condone it.[95]

In South Africa, especially among the Bapedi and Zulu tribes, child marriage is customary and forced, called by the Bapedi tribe 'go thiba difate' and by the Zulu tribe 'ukuganisela.' The Customary Marriage Act 120 of 1998 does not give the child enough protection as they cannot speak for themselves when their parents make marriage decisions on their behalf. Forced child marriages rob the girl of her human rights, including education.[96]

---

[95] www.irishtimes.com.news/world/dontcallitchildmarriage-itispaedophilia Article 8 July 2019 - downloaded April 2021.
[96] Sabinet News, Article by Velani Mtshali, Published 1 January 2014 – downloaded April 2021.

Marital rape within the confines of child brides:

There is a curiously loud silence on the subject of sexual conduct or behaviour between husband and wife in an abusive marriage, as in many cultures it is taboo to talk about. The trauma of constant humiliation causes the victim to lose sight of God and they struggle to reclaim human dignity. Marital rape has been labelled as the most serious violations of a woman's bodily integrity, in this case child bride cruelty and yet is a term that many people have a problem comprehending, with some describing it as 'a contradiction of terms' as the husband has a right to have sex with his spouse and age is not a factor.

Child bride, victim perspective:

Victims of child abuse could develop Stockholm Syndrome (SS) and the abuser makes the child believe it is 'God's will' for them to marry. They also coax the child to believe that they need to submit under their husband's authority. Ultimately, SS means loyalty and attachment to abusers, based in fear.

Girls who marry very young are at greater risk of heart attacks, cancer, diabetes, strokes and psychological disorders. They have a 50% or higher rate of dropping out of school and a high risk of living in poverty and three times more susceptible to becoming victims of domestic violence. According to (Reiss: 2018), the only one that benefits from child marriage is the child's parents financially and the paedophile who can 'legally' continue to abuse her, which in other countries would be termed as statutory rape. She goes on to say that in many ways human trafficking and child marriages are interchangeable terms.

In Florida, USA it is legal for a 40 year old man to marry a five year old girl. Girls a little older than 9 or 11 are shut silent about speaking out against it. (Reiss: 2018) states that the men marrying these girls, think the girls are 'old enough to marry' but not old enough 'to talk about it.'

Reiss herself was a child bride, as she put it 'The very act destroyed, and utterly and abruptly, ended my childhood and there was no escape.' Reiss now runs a shelter called *Unchained At Last* that assists child brides to escape.[97]

Many religions plays a large role in traditions and customs, endorsing child marriage.

Empowerment of young girls at risk of child marriage

Among various educational programs that can empower girls at risk of child marriage, more such topics include life skill straining, provision of safe spaces, discussions about marriage and sexuality, future intervention options and support networks.

---

[97]   https://www.theguardian.com/inequality/2018/feb/06/it-put-an-end-to-my-childhood-the-hidden-scandal-of-us-child-marriage

Girls are empowered if they are able to learn a skill that will develop their livelihood and increase their home economy. Support groups will assist them to overcome isolation.

Promoting education of young girls at risk of child marriage

The more education a girl can get, the less likely she is going to marry, or become a slave to a paedophile husband. Secular and Christian education will help her take care of herself.

Strategies to assist in child bride education are as follows:

- Legislative advocacy efforts to make education free and available and compulsory.
- Capitalise on the window of opportunity between puberty and the time of the arranged marriage, by providing substantive skills enhancing education.
- Address the needs of the girls and make them aware of their rights to education and the Act in place, to protect them.
- Keep girls in school for as long as possible.
- Education policies to include cutting down school fees, building more classrooms, providing grants and bursaries and stipends, free text books, uniforms, travel costs or correspondence distance learning.
- Providing grants for young married girls, provided they stay in school.

- The Act to be changed giving young girls the basic right to education until they turn 18.
- Pastors to gain counselling skills to educate their congregation members and not use their marriage license to marry child brides to older men.

Fathers marrying their daughters, pedophilia and incest

(Carl Jung developed this theory in 1913) The term describing a girl between the tender ages of 3 and 6 falling in love with her father and being sexually attracted to him is called The Electra Complex, the term of father falling in love with his own child is called The Oedipus Complex. Incest is strictly prohibited and opposed by God.

8.10 The Posthumous or Ghost Marriage.

Posthumous marriages became legal in France by Article 171 of the Civil Code. This law authorises solemnization, allowing the living to marry corpses. However, evidence must exist indicating that the deceased intended to marry while alive, the person prior to their death.

In China in 2013 four men were arrested for stealing female corpses to sell for posthumous marriages, the demand for dead wives is high enough for people to commit crimes such as murder, to make money out of it.[98]

In South Africa, there was one case of a man Jabulani Dlungwane from Durban, who married his fiancé Sindisiwe Khumalo two weeks after her death, to honour her wishes.

The second posthumous marriage in South Africa happened in 2004 when a man shot his pregnant girlfriend, then turned the gun on himself. The family of the couple preferred to remember them in happier times, so arranged their wedding for the same day as their funeral.[99]

Some posthumous marriages are consummated by necrophiles. The posthumous marriages that took place in South Africa, were not.

---

[98] Insider.com/horrifyingMarriageTraditions – Downloaded April 2021.
[99] East Coast Radio Interview and Article written by Damon Beard, 12 June 2018 – Downloaded April 2021.

Chapter 9   PUBLIC OUTCRY

9.1 The taxpayer outcry and points of view

In South Africa it currently costs over R10 000.00 ($800) monthly, to house a prisoner, considering his / her food, rehabilitation programs, water, electricity, warden's salaries, social workers salaries, education and prison apparel. Added to this the policeman's salary, the justice court systems and salaries, which is all funded by Government and in turn by the 'taxpayer!' Public funds support education for offenders, although it is clear that the bulk of the costs are spent on detention and not on rehabilitation or education.

The taxpayer's negative, yet *positively argumentative* outcry of why free education in prisons remains available to the incarcerated, refers to the 'lock them up and throw away the key' approach, while the church responds, 'Jesus is the key that sets them free.'

Social workers, educationists, psychologists cost money to employ, which most offenders take the opportunities presented of having, for granted. Most prison ministry leaders offering Christian education are unpaid, volunteers who deem the initiative as a privilege to serve God, offering their own time, money and educational materials and resources. Volunteers are not paid by The Department of Correctional Services in South Africa as well as the rest of Africa, they rely on unpaid volunteers, except for a petrol stipend, which deters those who cannot afford to give their services full time. Most volunteers during the week are retired people, who may not conduct prison ministry after the age of 65, for safety reasons. This is not always ideal, as juvenile offenders connect on a better level with younger prison ministry leaders. In many different prisons in the USA, Canada, Portugal, Italy and Australia for instance, prison ministry is a full time paid position and funding is plentiful.

The programs attended in prison by offenders, are always accompanied by certificates, which is their aim to achieve, not always because they have a deep seeded interest in getting to know God, or change their lives or behavioural patterns, but for the purposes of the parole board granting them an early exit from prison. In many instances, prisoners have been found to 'pretend' they are Christian, while still choosing to be part of the gangs, because they know as a Christian you get the privilege of sleeping safely in the 'Brothers Room' and attend many programs which means less time in their cells, with the possibility of eating good food if the spiritual workers from organisations are allowed to bring platters or similar to the programs.

Prison is termed as the 'Devil's playground.' During April (Easter), December and January (Christmas and New Year Season) the prisons have introduced an initiative called 'Operation Vala' which constitutes bringing in snooker tables, darts, finger bagatelles, chess, drafts and other games.

The suicide rate in prison is horrendous during these periods, along with the gang rivalry and the 'games' are considered a distraction and attraction to keep the prisoner's minds occupied, which produces excellent lower suicide rate results. During this period, many wardens are on leave so there is only skeleton staff, so keeping the prisoners busy is also a form of better control in this hostile environment. For any member of the public, who could be a visitor and does not understand this concept, their first impression of seeing Operation Vala in action could be an attitude of outrage, *'Prison is a holiday camp! And they are holidaying on my tax money!'*

While playing games are fun, they also encourage coordination development skills, thinking on your feet, forward planning and thinking, competitiveness and an environment of possibly making peace with your enemies.

In Goulburn Prison, Melbourne, Australia a new 'Super-Maximum' prison called 'Prison City' is currently being built, costing AUS$1.2Billion. An all-male prison with a more normalized rehabilitation living environment, including coffee shops, barber shops, a chapel, skills development program classrooms, sport facilities, etc. which many Australian tax payers are horrified at, as Prison City sounds more like a free holiday camp, than a punishment center, build and run on their hard earned money.

In the USA the recidivism rate is 40% for those offenders who have not attended educational programs, but only 12% for those who have, thus a definitive correlation between education and recidivism (Slater: 1994), saving the tax payer money.

The taxpayer, aka critics, see education for offenders as a waste of time and money, whereas the money could be better spent on assisting the victims of crime and their families. Taxpayers also argue that people will offend, in order to be given the opportunity for free board and lodging and education. Most citizens feel that offenders should be harshly punished in exchange for the harsh crimes administered on the taxpayers themselves. To enhance the offender's life on the taxpayer's and the victims of crimes monies, is inconceivable and unforgiveable. (Bracken: 2011) affirms that prisoners have a negative attitude towards education and work, as more than half of them were unemployed prior to committing their crime and only 80% of them have literacy skills.

Even though educational programs are not compulsory yet in South African prisons, recidivism is deemed best achieved through development and correction, not through punishment. The Department of Correctional Services take the approach that every human being is capable of change, if offered the right opportunity.

It boils down to more than just crime prevention and intervention, but includes social justice, empowerment through education, social responsibility, inclusion of community projects and prison ministry, correction of offender behaviour patterns, human development and social values. Education in prison is cost effective and provides substantial return as an investment, for society. Harsh prison sentences, with no form of education, could be a recipe for a higher level of recidivism.

During this research it was discovered that in South African prisons, completing matric is free, but all other secular education is <u>not</u> free, which most tax payers are not aware of. Some Christian programs however, are free but some are paid for by their families, friends or bursaries that they obtain.

Sadly, a sensitive issue remains, prisoners on death row, obtain no opportunities for study or educational programs and often sit in a 3 meter x 3 meter cell with no books, radio or anything else allowed, but just their dark tormenting thoughts. Study for someone who is doomed to die, is a waste of time and money in the prison system.

9.2 The Butterfly effect.

There is a butterfly effect to pedophilia and necrophilia, in that the detrimental choices made by just one man can shake a nation.

And yet, there is a positive butterfly effect that can emerge, from the tragedy thereof.

The choices we make affect others, whether we recognise it, admit it, or not. One such example is the crime committed by Mortimar Saunders, the Elsie's River man, who by way of premeditated thoughts, poisoned three year old Courtney Pieters, with ant poison and then beat her, chocked her and placed a towel over her mouth, to stop her from screaming. He raped and killed her, because he was angry at her mother Juanita Pieters. He then had sexual intercourse with her corpse, then broke every bone in her body so that her corpse could be fitted into a plastic bag, after which he dumped her body in an open plot of land amid the nearby factories in Epping Industria. Her body was only found nine days after she was reported missing.[100] He received a fifty year prison sentence. Although he apologised to her mother, as well as his own family during his trial, he denied raping her while she was alive and only admitted to necrophilia. However forensic pathologist Professor Dempers, testified that in his findings during the autopsy, proved otherwise in that Courtney was raped twice prior to her death and endured much torture. Mortimar was aware that if he was found guilty for necrophilia, he would only receive a two year sentence, coupled with a few more years for poisoning Courtney. Only two years into his sentencing he applied for leave to appeal, which was an unsuccessful attempt.

---

[100] ewn.co.za downloaded 23 March 2021.

The butterfly effect of this is the public's outrage. The community blamed the mother as she had a reputation for leaving the child alone in his care regularly, or in the care of the other children in the family to watch over Courtney. The fear was mob justice, the community members wanted to attack Juanita Pieters. At the time of her murder, Courtney was in the care of her six year old brother, which in itself has a lifetime traumatic effect on his psyche.

Besides the mob justice, the public are petitioning for the death penalty to be reinstated for aggravated rapists and murderers, paedophiles and necrophiles. Christian education advocacy is far removed from this equation. The public have a right to be angry, but do they have a right to revenge? (*Romans 12:19*) Revenge belongs to God.

9.3 Taboos and monetary economic consequences.

Taboos are a vital part of any society. There are economic consequences for taboos, enforced by social punishment, the most familiar of these being members of society. For this punishment to be effective, the behaviour patterns of the perpetrators needs to be observable. How does one determine right punishment for someone with 'dirty thoughts or desires' as thoughts are not evident. Social punishment could however, be self-inflicted.

In the same manner, 'to attach a monetary value to one's friendship or one's children or one's loyalty to one's country, is to disqualify one from certain social roles. People feel that making such an evaluation demonstrates that one is not a true friend, or parent, or citizen.'[101]

Taboos such as necrophilia are prohibited by laws in certain countries, the transgressions of which could lead to severe punishment, or as is the case in South Africa, only two years sentencing. In every country there are difference social laws that govern and restrict social behaviour patterns. Some taboos provide positive advantages to society, such as refraining from cannibalism, keeps the community safe from witnesses this atrocity or being eaten.

Taboos form identities, which are apparent in the choice of taboo one decides on embarking and the laws pertaining to the country they reside in: homosexuality, trans-gendering, religious practises, financial fraud, trafficking humans and children, dietary restrictions, pornography, trade in human organs, necrophilia and pedophilia, swingers, among others. The strength of the taboo, is affected by those who deviate, or consider deviating from it.

---

[101] Journal of forensic research: Fiske and Tetlock: 1997.

Different societies may also differ in the levels of taboos allowed or not allowed, as well as the different levels of concern shown by individuals.[102] The strength of the taboo also changes with time.

A starving person may benefit from eating a food considered taboo, thus evident that the person violating the taboo observes devotion to his/her own private benefits of the taboo. An example of this would be Peruvians eat guinea pigs and rats, or Chinese eat dogs, cats and snakes, most of which is considered taboo in South Africa. Yet there are some people groups residing in South Africa who will eat a snake, or rat.

Every deed starts with a thought, which grows into an idea, which cultivates into a decision, which transforms into an action. Thoughts are important to us as human beings, we enjoy thoughts, yet other thoughts that make us afraid we try to supress. We care about the thoughts of others and we care about what they think of us. We care about others knowing what we are thinking. We have limited control over our thoughts and changing them is often not easy. Many of our thoughts are taboo. God knows every thought and where every thought pattern will lead, which could affect our behaviour pattern and ultimately lead us down a path of destruction.

---

[102] Fessler and Navarette: 2003, 'For evidence on individual's variations in terms of emotions such as fear, anger, disgust or acceptance, in reaction to taboo stimuli.'

Knowing right from wrong, we do not act on taboo thoughts, but try to steer them in other directions or erase them.

Talking about taboos is speaking about the unthinkable, it should be obvious as part of characterisation, that it is wrong behaviour. But, it is only termed wrong behaviour depending on 'who' is talking about it.

Taboos cost money - as actions and choices, determine wealth gained or wealth wasted.

9.4 The Law of Consent as education

'Consent' is a law in Australia, a simple word to understand that when it comes to sex, how the words *YES* or *NO* would become clear enough? The federal government is trying to educate young Australians about the controversial topic of consent. The idea is that when a boy intends raping a girl, the word '*NO*' is not enough, it should be rather be '*UNLESS IT IS A YES, IT IS NOT A YES!*' Formal Consent Forms are made available to young people, to both sign before embarking on any sexual escapades. This method could also be criticized as being inflexible, for the fine and dividing line between real consent and mere submission, which may in retrospect cause greater complexity.

Many times drunk or drugged young girls at parties are raped, but no witnesses want to come forward to assist these victims. Abstinence from sex until marriage, is the biblical option, for Christian youth.

Launching websites and easily downloading Consent Forms should be made available to youth and in some cases, even adults. The effectiveness of this however, could be questioned in that a rapist could force a girl at gunpoint or any other compromising or threatening position, to sign the forms, in order that she cannot make a rape case against the perpetrator. There is, or may be, no consent in circumstances of fear, harm, threats, bodily harm, terror, force, mistaken identity, intimidation, coercion, extortion and fraud, deceit, intoxicating drug, alcohol or anaesthetic induced force. There is also no consent where the person in a 'position of authority or trust' of someone in their care, unlawful detainees, mentally ill, patients in a coma or unconscious, falsely led to believe that sex is used for hygienic or medical benefits, or animals.

A strategic approach needs to be followed and Consent Courses made available online, to educate law abiding citizens on what consent really means. There are experts that deliver proficient sexuality and relationship awareness programs and the secret to teaching these programs, could start with students from age of 4, where they learn to say 'NO' and know why they are saying NO. A perpetrator should not be able to 'avoid culpability' on the basis that 'they did not give any thought at all, as to whether the victim was consenting or not.'

If South Africa could adopt this law and national education campaign, to deter rape, gain respect among peers and making sex safer for all youth, it could provide legal clarity and educate the community about the boundaries of proscribed sexual behaviour.

The process of sexual abuse prevention does not start in a courtroom, it starts in a classroom. [103]

---

[103] YouTube Clip 60 Minutes Australia, Courageous Teenage Survivors of Sexual Assault Demanding Consent Education.

Chapter 10   WHAT RESPONSIBILITY DOES THE CHURCH HAVE?

10.1   The church's standpoint on Christian education, for sexual crimes

'Every church should be a bible school for its members,' says Pastor Maxwell Benjamin, Wellington.

One critical standpoint of the church, is that of gender based crimes, including sexual violence. Victim empowerment is the process by which individuals, churches, people groups and communities organise themselves to influence change, on the basis of their access to knowledge, political processes and financial, social and natural resources.

The church's approach should be to help deal with the *culture of silence* which should totally be eliminated, to enable victim empowerment. The 4 P's strategy could apply: *Prevention, Protection, Partnership and Programming*, which will strengthen the church's initiative as well as take up its role in eradicating sexual violence (C Bradley: 2004).[104]

---

[104] Justice not Silence, Churches facing sexual and gender based violence, EFCA Institute for Theological and Interdisciplinary Research, Published by Sun Press © 2013 Pages 182.

Prevention:	entails the economic empowerment of the victims
Protection:	includes speaking out, providing shelter and providing solutions for prevention of sexual violence, awareness campaigns
Partnership:	involves the church taking practical action to assist with rehabilitation and being aware of all sources of assistance for victims, shelters, counselling and stakeholders
Programs:	emphasises church or family members, holding dialogues or support groups, discussions and workshops, for victims and perpetrators

The church is best positioned to do the above, as it attracts people from all walks of life and can reach many with consistent messages and pre-existing structures that could be used to aid the struggle. Sexual abuse should be challenged by the church aggressively. Culture and tradition, religion and scripture, should not be misused to support or excuse sexual violence. Churches should take the lead in this fight and should engage all leaders, community members and stakeholders in addressing this mandate, by running programs and educating communities and transforming the world.

There is a lot of responsibility bestowed on the church and yet it has often been accused of being silent (Haddad 2003:155). The church possesses adequate tools to formulate theological justifications against sexual abuse and violence (Jonson 1998: 420). The church needs to construct and reconstruct its own biblical teachings regarding sexual sin and sexual violence.

Sexual violence is a private torture, described as comparable to having sex with a demon, not a human being.

10.2 Is the church willing to minister to the incarcerated?

Churches like so many other institutions, are undergoing changes, which compels them to take a wider view of their role in different communities they serve, including prisons, but often lack resources. Considering the fact that religion has to do with personal and social well-being, it would seem a natural consequence that the church needs to have a strong involvement in the study and practise of ministry among what the bible terms as *'whatever you did for one of the least of these, you did for me'* (Matthew 25: 40). Other Faith Based Organisations (FBO) and Christian Non-Profit Organisations (NPO) are generally known as meaningful role players, as an extended resource and voice to the church.

Different FBO's and NPO's have different focuses on different projects, to offer practical application and participation of the offender and ex-offender's diverse needs, which collaborated as a whole with the church, offers solutions, development and well-functioning. All FBO's and NPO's in this case, need to adopt a non-prescriptive, all-inclusive yet unique style of intervention, as a precondition.

Part of this style implies a willingness to reach out, listen, involve the community and family with the tangible issues and challenges the offenders face, in a non-demeaning manner, but rather empowers, builds dignity and self-respect. The prison stigma breaks down self-esteem and self-efficacy for the offender, because of the humiliation attached to people judging them.

For churches to minister to offenders, it needs to bring sensitisation into perspective, which is fundamental to authentic development. In the later work of Charles Elliot, he delivered the most profound critique of the church's project system, where he argued that the church needs nothing less than an uncritical imitation and embracement of Western modernised paradigm of social development. Sensing the need to train missionaries, that started off with no theological training, but expected to produce results, he put the church under great pressure to pick up programs, plans and ideas wherever they could. For varied reasons, they found these among the secular world, government driven programs, coupled with government funding.

These projects, Elliot termed as 'engines of growth' and 'pedagogy of the oppressed' which brought about social changes. Yet, inherent to this modus operandi, was the belief that certain societies were not suitable to achieve the level of growth, or be beneficiaries of the privileges that were idealised, which led to higher crime rates and increased recidivism, among other things such as poverty and inequality.

Traditionally, culturally and historically, church have proven helpful in social development, its mission to improve the lives of victims, alleviate poverty, counsel the hurting, heal the sick, cast out demons, feed the hungry and last but <u>not</u> least, minister to the incarcerated offenders. The basic perception is that offenders can find solace and comfort in turning to the church for interventions and enjoy the dynamics of empowerment. Many churches are slowly narrowing the gap of the unemployment rate, when the offender gets released, as Christians are more susceptible to giving grace and forgiveness and second chances, than the secular world is.

Empowerment is one of the most valuable by-products of social development for individual offenders and prisons and corporates. Without empowerment, successes may reflect as questionable. Acts of misdemeanour in order to survive, may take dishonourable forms, such as petty crime, dishonesty, pilfering goods and even prostitution and will be seen by society as having no scruples or good morals.

This shame and humiliation of the offender could lead to alienation, isolation, self-loathing, interpersonal and relational problems, conflict, unforgiveness and anger. By being empowered and supported to find new coping mechanisms, they can arrive at constructive, sustainable and amicable solutions. In situations like these, the church is a cohesive factor in strengthening ties, helping them to determine their value and reach the potential God has for their futures. Relational projects stand at the heart of 'mission' of churches and such projects represent reconciliation, restitution, restoration, liberation and justice and marginalising sub-cultures within a national society being brought into creative, rather than destructive interaction, within the body of Christ.

The definition of collaboration is, 'The relationship between stakeholders pooling resources together, in order to meet the objectives that neither could meet independently.'

There are three roles the church plays for this endeavour, the first being embracing social development, the second the issue of healing and empowerment, the third the needs of organisations and the church to collaborate, not just locally, but worldwide. Working jointly, could provide stumbling blocks or acceptance of differences and reaching agreements in common vision, goals and a sense of hope.

Collaboration is seen as principally relevant for the social development discourse, as through it the uneven degrees of power represented through the church, social workers, offenders, prison authorities and community leaders and members, are levelled out. The lack of capacity in numbers of skilled people in the church, would be the rationale for FBO's and NPO's to team up and undertake joint projects, to achieve mutually agreed and beneficial outcomes. The advantages of learning from one another, sharing experiences and opportunities and contributing towards a better understanding, empowers all parties involved. The meaning of collaborative relational projects does not lie in the quantum of their efforts, but rather in their ability to influence the thinking, behavioural patterns and the attitudes of the offenders.

By accepting this challenge and becoming facilitators in empowering, the church has a distinctive role to play. The church has an important function, which is instrumental in changing people's lives, a positive tool for changing mind sets, seeking new ways to become significant participants in the transformation of offenders and ex-offenders. The church faces the inescapable responsibility to undertake sustainable and collaborative impact.[105]

---

[105] Religion and Social development in Post-Apartheid South Africa, Perspectives for Critical Engagement, Chapter 2 by Anna Nieman, Published by Sun Press © 2010 Pages 37-43, 247.

Collaborations:

Collaborations for churches to assist sexual crime offenders or sex addicts, could include organisations and support groups such as: Cocaine Anonymous, Al-Anon, Co-Dependents of Sex Addicts Anonymous, Emotions Anonymous, International Institution for Trauma, National Council for Family Recovery, Runaway and Suicide Hotline, Sex and Love Addicts Anonymous, Sexual Addiction Resources / Dr Patrick Carnes, Sexual Compulsives Anonymous, Sexaholics Anonymous, Society for the Advancement of Sexual Health, CABSA for HIV/Aids and other sexual diseases, Survivors of Incest Anonymous, Networking for Christ SA: Anger and Forgiveness, Centre for Disease Control and Prevention and The Pink Ladies for Missing Persons.

Some recommended books to assist perpetrators and victims:

Mending a Shattered Heart, Women Who Love Sex Addicts, Healing Together, Sex Lies and Forgiveness, Rebuilding Trust, Sexuality and Depression Recovery, Is it Love or is it Addiction? Healing the Child Within, The Courage to Heal, Abused Boys, Victim no Longer, Silently Seduced, Pregnant by Daddy, The Courage to Change, Masquerade: What Mask am I hiding behind? She has a Secret and My Father's Sexual Hunger and Understanding Necrophilia.

10.3 Responsible ethics approach to the formation of moral judgements.

Taking serious the problems we face in our communities and personal lives, needs thorough analysing to conclude responsible ethics. Part of accurate analysing includes historical content and context of the problem at hand, as well as future prospects of alternative actions that bring moral solutions.

To most of society necrophilia for instance, is taboo, morally incorrect and for the most part, deemed disgusting. In a world of responsible ethics, virtues and values have lost their domination in all spheres of life. Distortion of morals express discrimination and are scrutinised for their non-applicability perspectives, depending on who is judging. With pedophilia, moral norms include not exposing children to sexual activity too early in their development, while paedophile rings argue the point of who said sex is not good for a child, or that the paedophile is not in love with the child he is grooming and molesting? To be considered, is that often good intentions, could have exasperating consequences.

Responsible ethics obliges people to make deliberate decisions in the face of ethical problems. Encroaching transformation of justification and bureaucratisation, have opened the doors that result in diminishing room for acting in accordance with one's own ethical convictions, which could be the consequence of acting in fear or ignorance.

Moral codes are the core components of the Christian faith, how social and conventional decisions are made and can be seen as part of cultural and social structures that underpin morality (Broom 2003:164ff). Humans are free to develop new morals, however this carries great responsibility and should not be delegated to 'objective divine moral codes' as is demonstrated through the Ten Commandments and Jesus' last command to mankind, which are historically revealed as former or latter, even though over time they have acquired authority and biblical truth.

One's morals are foundationally built on historical social contexts and evolutionary pasts. We are therefore constrained, but not determined by our historical past, which shows that our moral awareness has progressed and will not be fixed forever as unchangeable entities.[106]

---

[106] Living Theology, Essays presented to Dirk J. Smit, Published by Bible Media 2013 © Pages 468 – 479 written by Etienne de Villiers.

Chapter 11   CHAPLAINCY   INFLUENCE   ON CHRISTIAN EDUCATION IN PRISONS

11.1 Prison institution and prison chaplaincy's endorsement of Christian educational programs.

Chaplains who serve prisons have an incredible opportunity to promote educational programs to assist offenders, as Chaplains are a life-saving source of Jesus' grace. Christian educational programs that depict God's unconditional love, acceptance and redemption, serve to influence and encourage.

In South African prisons, the Chaplain's main function is to provide free exercise of religion to offenders, to walk a road with them in the Christian context, challenging them to make better choices for a better life and supplying them with the moral tools to do so, through educational programs. They support offenders, especially when their family members and friends have forsaken them and they have no moral or monetary provision from outside. The Chaplain is a calm, stabilizing force whose roles vary, depending on the institution they are serving. They minister to offenders, their families and victims of crime. Chaplains depend on the direction of the Holy Spirit, to discern the most effective way and correct time to counsel and witness.

The Chaplain has the 'power' to decide and endorse which programs, volunteers and organisations may do prison ministry in their prison. Rehabilitation and reduction of sentence efforts, include finding alternate ways of penalising, such as community service or halfway houses. These efforts, which comprise of four components namely retribution, deterrence, incapacitation and rehabilitation, have not yet reached the desired results. Prison chaplaincy makes a valuable contribution to restoring dignity and humanity, the aim being the holistic restoration of human beings. Alternatives to prison need more nuance than what is currently being delivered. Diversion programs should be designed to deter prison sentences, contributing to social and personal development, while the perpetrator wears an electronic GPS tracker, strapped to their ankles, for monitoring purposes.

The environment that chaplains work in consist of a variety of different religions (different spiritual maturity levels), traditions, races, cultures and age groups. This often poses a challenge for the chaplain to preserve his personal integrity and beliefs, while being exposed to other belief systems. Studies conducted by (Skotnicki 2008:139), religion can facilitate a conversion experience and the formation of a new identity. The essence of religion includes the willingness to change and grow, even whilst being incarcerated.

Prison chaplains provide opportunities for marginalised groups to speak and make their voices heard in the prisons. They provide platforms for differences to be acknowledged, understood and used creatively to knit a common story from different threads, which is not an easy task. The work of the chaplain facilitates breaking down barriers, closing gaps, binding people together, healing wounds and restoring relationships with family members as well as community members, in particular victims of crime, without forcing their own values and beliefs on others. There is power in listening to, advocating for and working with others, promoting acceptance, unity and love. The emotional sentiments of prisoner's stories are factual and genuine. While incarcerated the chaplains seek to give prisoners the best opportunities for spiritual growth and transformation, to receive encouragement, counselling and education from wise and caring people.

Religious beliefs have the power to deter criminal and delinquent behavioural patterns and acts, but only when supported by strong bonds and networks, which chaplains provide through allowing prison ministry and Christian educational programs to be run in the prisons, through the creating and strengthening of external support systems beyond the prison walls.

Some religious organisations encourage teachings and practises that are helpful and meaningful to offenders that face prison culture challenges. However, Chaplains should always be aware of which educational programs will bring healing or harm to the offender. The chaplain's role is not to 'fix' offenders, but to create the safe space platform for healing and positive change to take place.

Intervention programs that focus on fear or shame inmates, such as the television series 'Scared Straight' where troubled youth are intimidated by older prisoners, have a history of not working in the long run. God does not work through fear, but instead through love. Self-help programs may only impact one offender at a time and don't seem to stick with helping them long term. Programs focused on teaching specific skills and techniques which help offenders to manage specific situations, do make a difference. (Brault 2014: 3) suggests that programs designed to be put in practise outside of prison, may be forgotten by the time the offender is released, losing its effectiveness along the way.

Programs that focus on anger management, grief, decision making, coping skills, problem solving, self-control and forgiveness, from a religious perspective are very effective. Many offenders distrust authority and have a history of abusive behaviour.

Theological reflection on issues of faith, serve as an instrument to preserve, nurture and support change in the offender's life, behaviour and attitude.

In a study conducted by (Schneider and Feltey 2009:443), it was found that religious studies conducted by incarcerated women, that were locked up for life for murder, found 'freedom within' when they accepted Christ. This freedom played an integral role in their healing and ability to reconstruct their lives. Women need acceptance, love and nurturing, which is what they found in Christ's redemption, giving them renewed hope. Relationship with God, not fancy religious practises, is key.

In South African prisons, chaplaincy is generally structured on a 'one size fits all' paradigm. Christianity is the religion that predominates prisons, with Islamic teachings following close behind. Christian educational programs should be made available to all offenders, regardless of their faith, without forceful application.

Chaplaincy and pastoral care for people who have been released from prison is sorely lacking, due to lack of finances and other resources. Without support, the offender adjusting and reintegrating becomes difficult, especially if their studying of programs stops on release.

Organisations like Nehemiah Bible Institute and Networking for Christ SA, provide offender with free Christian programs even after discharge. (Paget and McCormick 2006:11) depict it perfectly, '*A ministry of presence is in itself an important intervention.*' If incarceration is not only seen as punishment, but as rehabilitation, the success of it would result in reducing recidivism, positive behaviour, repentance, forgiveness and reconciliation.

11.2 Evidence of influence or non-influence of Christian educational programs and FBO volunteers

From the perspective of humanism, Christian education promotes virtues such as patience, kindness, love, compassion, forgiveness, benevolence and care. Through a proper educational opportunity, individuals who lack knowledge and skills may find themselves on the wrong side of the law, however through faith based volunteers, can still be taught relevant life, economic, social skills and moral norms and respect for humanity and their property.

These values seek to redirect and rehabilitate offenders to become better humans, build strong foundational moral philosophies and ethical reasoning. The knowledgeable guiding principles and wisdom absorbed in a Christian reflective approach, to education, cannot be lost as they become part of the offender's integral self. The faith based volunteers become mentors, stand in mothers and fathers, older brothers or sisters, playing a crucial part in the positive influence of the offender's life. Sensitivity needs to be exercised, because should the volunteer that mentored and assisted the offenders, suddenly drop out of the program, the offender experiences rejection, slight depression and feelings of abandonment, once again putting their guard up and tearing down the trust they built up, ultimately causing them to see God with the same view, a God who is sometimes there, but abandons them when they need him most. 'How can this person say they are a Christian, yet hurt me so deeply?'

Caution means, as a volunteer is to strongly recommended to always point the offender to Christ, not to man, as man will always disappoint, but God never will' (*Jeremiah 17: 5-6*).

Prison Chaplains hold quarterly meetings and invite all the FBO's and NPO's volunteers to attend. In these meetings educational items are discussed, such as offenders who do not attend school, or which educational programs are being run, mentorship, access to prison dates, times and duration of classes, palliative care, pastoral care, hospice care, counselling, progress reports, letters of good standing, finances and educational program performance indicators.

Through Christian education, offenders learn to evaluate themselves and find that they want to change for the better, even hardened gangsters have been moved to tears.

11.3 Community Policing Forum

Several communities in South Africa hold a monthly forum meeting in the Town Hall, involving police officers, community leaders, NPO and FBO's, security companies, correctional services officers, shop owners and general members of the public that would like to voice their concerns over circumstances and happenstances in their close areas.

Items discussed include gang activity, school children, community complaints, parolees soon to be released into community, NPO's and FBO's that will take responsibility to mentor parolees, NPO's and FBO's that will take responsibility to run educational programs based on life skills, social skills and assist with job seeking for parolees.

Mr Ulrich Lottering, who is also Managing Director of Networking for Christ South Africa (NFCSA), NPO, works with educational programs with offenders and ex-offenders, victims of crime, development skills for employment opportunities for ex-offenders, drug rehabilitation, life skills, other ex-inmate aftercare services. (NFCSA) also offers counselling at Police Stations for victims of Gender Based Violence.

Would it not save the tax payer money, to know the offender will not return to prison, but find an employment opportunity to earn his own and in the interim, pay his own taxes, benefitting another offender that is still incarcerated?

Mr Lottering also serves as Chairman of the monthly Wellington Policing Forum, states that 'These forums would be beneficial to all communities in South Africa, as it promotes peace, informs the community in advance which offenders that committed crimes are soon to be released, to give concerned citizens an opportunity to have a voice. If they vote that the parolee cannot safely be let back into the community, or that the victim feels unsafe having the offender out of prison, the prison parole board will be formally notified and the prisoner will be apprehended. When solid proof of having attended Christian education programs has been presented, as well as proof of transformation and victim mediation, the community will reconsider the offender's release.'

11.4 Accredited versus non-accredited secular and Christian education

More evidence is surfacing of bursaries being made available to offenders, with accredited training providers and training programs.

Accredited Education	Non-Accredited Education
Learning program must meet or exceed standard set by South African Qualification Authority (SAQA) requirements	Non-formal (adult learning) which is structured, taught learning which has no need to meet set out requirements
Accreditation indicates that the training is of a high quality and has excellent and proficient policies and procedures in place	Training can take place that is not in accordance with policies and procedures, but rather in what they believe is right
Prisons can benefit through mandatory grant claims as part of their annual Workplace Skills Plans and Annual Training Reports	No mandatory grant claims as part of annual Workplace Skills Plans and Annual Training Reports.
Prisons using accredited training programs, contribute towards their BEE scoring	Does not contribute towards BEE scoring
Will enhance career development and achievement for higher salary or position	Will enhance knowledge, but not career development and achievement for higher salary or position

Certificate of Competence can be issued	Certificate of Attendance can be issued
Assessment, Moderation, Certification and RPL applies	No Assessment, Moderation and RPL applies
Learnership can be applied for directly from relevant Seta or other governing body	Learnership cannot be applied for directly from Seta or other governing body
Credits can be awarded towards qualification	No credits can be awarded, does not lead to a qualification

11.5 RPL Processes based on accredited secular and Christian education

Recognised Prior Learning (RPL) is based on an idea that we each hold a wealth of information, life and work experiences that could be relevant towards a qualification that we are striving towards and studying for. RPL allows us to give credit for knowledge and skills from experience gained over the years, without the official qualification studies, thus they may need to complete just part of the studies to meet the requirements for the full qualification. How or where the knowledge was gained does not matter, as long. As what was learned can be linked to the units of competency for the qualification and the level of competency can be proved, will suffice for the prerequisites of the credits seeked by the applicant.

RPL usually involves:

- Previous study, formal and informal
- Work experience, paid, unpaid, practical, technical, academic
- Life experience, years, broader picture

RPL can be granted for part qualification, or awarded for full qualification. Offenders should be informed of the option to apply any development skills and training they obtained in prison, to have the right to apply for RPL.

The following principles should be met:

- What are permissible forms of evidence
- What qualifications are available through the relevant competency standards
- What competency standards will be assessed
- Method of appealing an unfavourable decision

The process should be transparent:

- The intent of the assessment
- Exactly which aspects will be assessed
- How the assessment will proceed and unfold
- Which criteria will be used to judge performance

Offenders or ex-offender to provide evidence for Portfolio of Evidence (POE). Below are recommended strategies for the information that needs to be supplied:

Direct	Observation Simulations Demonstrations Role Play
Indirect	Documents Certificates Third party responses Work/Skills samples Projects
Supplementary	Questions Tests Assessments Reports / Results Hypotheticals Oral presentation

Third Party responses are anyone who can testify to the quality and quantity of work and development skills that will assist the process of RPL application. A third party report is not sufficient by itself, but adds value to other evidence in the indirect category.

If an applicant can prove their competency, the delivery plan can be executed.

RPL should typically be discussed with:

- Supervisors
- Volunteer teachers
- Prison teachers
- Prison authorities
- Spiritual Care Workers
- Candidates (offenders)
- Trainers and Assessors

If the offender's claim for recognition of Christian educational competency is accompanied by the appropriate proof, this will satisfy the requirement for evidence and the RPL qualification will be granted.

11.6 Social Workers and Psychologists influence on education and rehabilitation

Social Workers in South Africa are not trained specifically on rehabilitating offenders, as their qualifications are obtained from the private sector learning environment, which does not cater for prisons. There are also no 'Forensic' Psychologists. Criminal Profiling is not a specific job in South Africa, but merely a portion of a Psychologist's job specification. In order to qualify to rehabilitate offenders, a Social Worker would have to do a series of other short courses, to make them a subject expert.

Similar to South African Policemen, Social Workers and Psychologists are often traumatised and need counselling themselves, when working closely with offenders that have committed dreadful crimes. Social Workers and Psychologists can make recommendations for the necessary Christian and secular educational programs required for offenders, based on the outcomes of the counselling sessions.

The Chaplain continues the process, arranges the programs, volunteers and offenders, based on the recommendations made by the Social Workers and Psychologists. Volunteers from FBO's and NPO's run the prison 'database approved' programs only.

No awaiting trial prisoners may attend any educational programs or receive counselling until sentencing has taken place.

Social Workers and Psychologists also analyse offenders and make recommendations for parole, based on parole conditions. In South Africa, once an offender goes on parole, they are on parole for life.

Social Workers and Psychologists, especially at maximum security prisons are always on high alert and at risk of being stabbed or killed by gangsters. Safety and security are imperative for their protection and need counselling for these hostile environment actions.

11.7 Prison database approval of Christian educational programs.

No FBO's or NPO's can run programs in prison, without first registering their specific programs on the Department of Correctional Services (DCS) database, as a registered Service Provider.

The procedure entails completing the application forms, attaching the required documents. Failure to comply with the DCS requirements, will constitute no entry into prison to teach any educational programs. Once the forms have been processed by the prison clerk, they will invite the FBO's and NPO's volunteers to give a presentation to a panel of about 10 members of DCS staff, which will represent at least 3 or more prisons in the local area. Included in the panel are the Heads of Prisons, Spiritual Care Workers, Chaplains, Social Workers and Psychologists. Presentation of the program the FBO's and NPO's offer offenders, could consist of physical facilitator manuals, workbooks, Power-point presentations, materials and pamphlets depicting the ministry and program history and impact.

After the presentation, the panel will ask questions and based on the answers provided, the application will be approved or not approved. The DCS may request changes to be implemented before approval and they may not approve for reasons of non-compliance.

Notification of acceptance onto the prison database, is a process that takes a few weeks, or months. This application has to be renewed or updated every 3 years.

Training of the volunteers is also important, as working in an intense prison environment is different to working in other public schools or churches.

Chapter 12   RECOMMENDED SOLUTIONS FOR EX-OFFENDERS TO SUCCEED

In Australia, there is a mini-town on the outskirts of a main town, called Pervert Park. This is a caravan park, with a few built houses, a community with a high wall all around it. Living in this park, are exclusively paedophiles, to the rest of society, total outcasts. The paedophile offenders may not live or work or shop within a certain radius of children, schools, malls, etc. They form a weekly support group for therapy, run by a non-practicing paedophile.[107]

As he explains, as some priests choose to keep themselves celibate, he chooses to do the same, rather than harm or damage a child emotionally. He also counsels other pedophiles worldwide, who struggle with this condition and do not desire to harm children, via his website. Living in Pervert Park, the paedophiles make a living for themselves through skills development, running their own home based businesses, some examples being electricians, bakers and mechanics, within their own 'village.'

Children are safe from them and the paedophiles are protected from angry mobs and being separated from children and have the support group to contact in weak moments. The paedophiles hold prayer meetings and ask God to help them not to commit offences against children.

---

[107] YouTube Clip – Pervert Park

Other countries could adopt the 'Pervert Park' concept, as it could be a solution beneficial to community members, family members, perpetrators and others, except it should have a positive connotation name change.

Some paedophiles are necrophiles too. Diversion programs are designed to assist society members to not offend at all, diverting them from prison to making better life choices. Most are aimed at young people, yet again, none of these programs specifically include assistance for necrophilia nor pedophilia.

12.1 Listed below, suggestions for possible solutions and suggested laws that can be implemented, which will positively affect educational streams and various issues involved in this book

Necrophilia

- Better management and monitoring of dead bodies and preservation measures
- Quicker burial for bodies
- Adult diversion programs
- Christian educational programs
- Cameras installed 24/7 in funeral homes and autopsy rooms
- Detect signs earlier, of psychiatric disorders among those working with corpses

- Raise more awareness of bacterial proliferation
- More stringent legal measures, more severe sentencing for necrophilia
- New laws instituted, to protect corpses
- Review of laws regulating cemeteries, burials, cremations, autopsy's, funeral parlors, embalming quarters, ambulances, and other places where corpses are present
- Train Pastors and Christian Counsellors as specialists for therapy for necrophilias and paedophiles, particularly in the area of diminished empathy anti-social personality disorder, moral rights and wrongs and depression
- Deliverance ministry aimed at pedophilia and necrophilia healing
- Freedom from use of drugs and alcohol, also needs to be taken into consideration
- Generate medications that alter the brain to repulse the odours of corpses
- Programs to be designed for 'Impulse control and decision making'
- Christian programs to put in place to specifically assist necrophiles, with teachers equipped with the correct knowledge to support and contribute towards healing and non-judgemental understanding of their dilemma and directing them to a functional foundation

of Christianity and a relationship with God.

- There are things to consider in a sexual offender treatment programs which have distinct disadvantages: necrophiles that discuss their crimes, may be triggered by the memories thereof and plan to reoffend (*Romans 7:5*).
- Just as he law forbids paedophiles to live or work in any environment within a certain radius of children, necrophiles should be forbid to work in any environment close to corpses, thus wear a GPS tracking device around their ankles or a microchip monitoring device medically incised, as a permanent structure of observing their movements, programmed to set off an alarm should they go near graveyards, funeral homes, mortuaries or the like.

Pedophilia

- More child protection measures to be instituted
- Christian programs to be put in place to specifically assist paedophiles, with teachers equipped with the correct knowledge to support and contribute towards healing and non-judgemental understanding of their dilemma and directing them to a functional foundation

of Christianity and a relationship with God.

- Government to make the antiandrogen 'chemical castration and hormonal agents treatment' that is administered every three months called 'Cyproterone or Depo-Provera' injections available, to lower sex drive and fantasies (lowering the perpetrator's testosterone levels dramatically) at no cost. Many paedophiles and necrophiles seek help, but cannot afford secular psychologists nor medications.
- Diversion and intervention programs should be designed to deter prison sentences
- Paedophiles to wears an electronic GPS trackers, or have a microchip monitoring device medically incised, as a permanent structure of observing their movements around child based environments
- The Department of Social Development, should make the Sex Offender Register information available to the public, especially on paedophiles.
- South Africa could adopt the 'Pervert Park' concept from Australia, as it could be beneficial to community members, family members and perpetrators, except it should have a positive connotation name change.

- Diversion and interventions programs to be designed, based on specific research for troubled teens who are deemed social outcasts, who have felt a strong urge to harm and kill animals, or kill people from a young age. More specialists to be trained with a sound understanding of issues relevant to sexual crime and killing necessary.
- There are things to consider in a sexual offender treatment program which have distinct disadvantages: paedophiles that discuss their crimes, may be triggered by the memories thereof and plan to reoffend (*Romans 7:5*).

Education, mentoring, employment

- Train prison officials to run programs within the prison penal system
- Churches and ministerial organisations, bible colleges, seminaries and bible institutes, should invest more in donating Christian programs or bursaries to prisons and offenders and pay stipends to pastors and prison ministry leaders to present them.

- Counselling offenders, with specialised expertise in the areas lacking of knowledge, such as necrophilia, pedophilia, marital rape, stalking, abuse of the elderly, etc. should be designed to be stimulating, healing, comforting and expressive.
- Pastoral care counsellors should be able to make recommendations and referrals for offenders to enhance their healing, in the area of their specific offence.
- The Department of Correctional Services should budget for program development, paying people qualified to write programs, for offenders.
- Government should consider putting aside study bursary monies annually for ex-offenders that show scholastic talent.
- The Department of Correctional Services should employ people that run diversion programs and post release programs for ex-offenders full time.
- Monthly policing forums would be beneficial to all communities in South Africa, as it informs the community in advance which offenders that committed which crimes are soon to be released, to give concerned citizens an opportunity to have a voice.

If they vote that the parolee cannot safely be let back into the community, or that the victim feels unsafe having the offender out of prison, the prison parole board will be formally notified and the prisoner will be apprehended. When solid proof of having attended Christian education programs has been presented, as well as proof of transformation and victim mediation, the community will reconsider the offender's release.[108]

- South African Police Departments should have community classrooms available at various community police stations for volunteers that conduct counselling or run programs for ex-offenders, where they can do so in a safe environment for all.

- South Africa could adopt the Consent Law and run national education campaigns, to deter rape, gain respect among peers and making sex safer for all youth. Launch websites and make easily available downloading of Consent Forms to youth and in some cases, even adults.[109]

---

[108] Mr Ulrich Lottering, Chairman of Wellington Policing Forum with Community Members and Managing Director of Networking for Christ South Africa, NPO.
[109] YouTube Clip 60 Minutes Australia, Courageous Teenage Survivors of Sexual Assault Demanding Consent Education.

- Annual prison ministry conferences and prison ministry expos, where prison ministries and related organisations can showcase their specialities, should be implemented in each province of South Africa, to support networking and integrating services.[110]
- To address the issue of prisoners being confused by all the different ministry backgrounds and teachings, A National Prison Ministry Governing Association should be established in South Africa, where all prison ministries should be registered and all volunteers officially trained and screened with a recognised universal prison ministry leadership program, accompanies by in-house training for specialised knowledge of the program they will be facilitating and presenting, before being accepted to minister to offenders. Volunteers should have a formal prison ministry leadership qualification and their certificate should be updated every three years, after they have attend a refresher course. Volunteers need to produce a police clearance record and even if they were offenders themselves, must still go through the normal process.

---

[110] Already instituted through Allandale Prison, Western Cape, in 2019.

All programs presented to the prison's database committee for service providers, must also be registered at the National Prison Ministry Governing Association, as well as registering the organisation represented. A three yearly fee should be charged for volunteers, while an annual fee should be charged per prison ministry organisation. The Department of Correctional Services should not accept any prison ministry or volunteer, not officially screened and registered. The National Prison Ministry Governing Association's website, should be designed to assist anyone in any area, seeking to get involved in prison ministry.

- South African Qualification Assurance (SAQA) should put a Designated Professional Body with relevant unit standards in place, for programs designed around rehabilitation of prisoners, crime and behavioural attitudes, including sexual crimes related to sexual offenders such as necrophiles and paedophiles, which should be compulsory to attend.

- South Africa could adopt the 'Prison City' concept from the 'Super-Maximum' Goulburn Prison, Melbourne, Australia, as it could be beneficial to community members, family members and perpetrators. An all-male prison with a more normalized rehabilitation living environment, including coffee shops, barber shops, chapel, bible school, healing program classrooms, sport facilities, etc. paves the way for social reintegration, restorative and skills development.
- Intervention programs should be implemented early in the offender's incarceration period and sometimes the program needs to be repeated 'until the penny drops' so to speak. (Tardif: 2007) states that sexual murderers with good cognitive abilities are quite capable of showing successful integration of treatment; and treatment should take place only where objective assessment processes are available.'
- All offenders who are skilled in a trade, or higher educational level than others, should be made facilitators of prison secular and Christian education training programs, to reduce cost and bypass red-tape processes.

- Intervention programs should be designed to assist Correctional Services staff working with sexual offenders, assisting them to understand these crimes and the offenders, assist with accurate assessments as well as professionalism and the risks of emotional involvement and provide counselling for the trauma they may experience.
- More empirical research should be done and more awareness campaigns launched, to educate the Zulu and Sepedi tribes, about early school dropouts, early age childbirth risks and trauma, and allowing children to physically develop into adults before sex, marriage and pregnancies.[111]
- More educational awareness needs to be expended in how men should treat women and women should treat men, which should include lessons on how adults should treat children.
- More educational intervention programs should be run in high schools for mothers and teen daughters, over unwanted pregnancies, especially due to the sexual crime of rape, or sex with no consent.

---

[111] Sabinet News, Article by Velani Mtshali, Published 1 January 2014 – downloaded April 2021.

- TVET Colleges could run vocational educational programs and specialised skill courses, assisting literate and non-literate ex-offenders with bursaries. Government should consider mandating TVET Colleges countrywide to fill minimum 10% of their student base with rehabilitated ex-offenders, or establishing a 100% ex-offender student TVET College where there are clusters of prisons, as a halfway rehabilitation centre, such as Wellington, Malmesbury, Tulbach, Paardeburg, Worcester and Paarl in South Africa, which consists of ten prisons in close proximity. Part of their curriculums should include social and life skills, basic work skills – with a balance of admin and practical application.
- Bible Schools and Institutions, as part of their tithing, should fill minimum 10% of their student base, presenting free Christian education to offenders and ex-offenders, giving them ministry, pastoral and missionary opportunities.

Recidivism

- Family members should be more involved with reintegration processes.
- Recidivism should be monitored and statistically accurately reported countrywide. There is a dire need, thus a new law should be put in place, with one central monitoring body, to accurately calculate and record recidivism rate percentage in South Africa, the task allocated to a South African Non-Profit Organization who works closely with pre and post release offenders, supported by The Department of Correctional Services, would be appropriate.
- The Department of Correctional Services should reach out to more businesses to employ ex-offenders in their areas, especially to prevent idleness while on parole.
- The needs of ex-offenders through broader research conducted, should not stop there, roll out action plans should be implemented and where niches exist, cavities should be filled.

- Mentors and counsellors should shadow ex-offenders and get to know their private world, in order to guide, discipline, reintegrate and rehabilitate them.[112]
- Government should put a law in place that all large companies consisting of 500 or more employees, should employ at least two ex-offenders of medium to lesser crimes, amid each 500. A company of 3,500 employees will thus employ 14 ex-offenders. Should a company consist of children, such as a school, where some ex-offenders cannot work, they should apply to the Government for exemption and instead, make an annual donation to a prison ministry organisation of their choice or to the National Prison Ministry Governing Association.
- Aftercare centres should be more structured and funded by Government, teaching proper skills development programs.
- Employment opportunities, with supervision, to be implemented for the offender to gain independence and a sense of dignity.

---

[112] Social Intelligence, The New Science of Human Relationships, book by Daniel Coleman (Published by Hutchinson, London, UK) © 2006 Page 296.

- Taxpayers should be made more aware that their taxes pay for incarceration, not education.

Chapter 13   BIBLICAL FOUNDATIONAL SUPPORT INFLUENCES

Just one word from God, is like a diamond, with seventy different facets. ~ Quote Jennifer

13.1 Biblical reference to necrophilia, pedophilia, harming children, death, sexual sin and soul ties and taboos

NECROPHILIA & DEATH

1 Kings 14:1-15

King Jeroboam's son Abijah fell ill and he told his wife to disguise herself and go to the Shiloh where the prophet Ahijah lives and to take ten loaves of bread, some cakes and a jar of honey, then to ask Abijah what will happen to their son. Ahijah told her that her husband and everyone in the city rejected God and worshipped idols and God was going to kill all the male members of their dynasty and who die inside the city will be eaten by dogs. However, her son Abijah will have a proper and dignified burial and the whole of Israel will mourn him, because he is the only one with whom the Lord is pleased.

When you live a life pleasing unto God, he will give you a dignified and proper burial. God loves you and cares about your body even after death. It is possible to ask God to allow you to die in a dignified manner and that your corpse will not be perversely abused after your death.

PEDOPHILIA / HARMING CHILDREN

Matthew 18:5-7

At that time the disciples asked Jesus who was the greatest in the kingdom of heaven. Jesus called a child and made him stand in front of them and said, 'I assure you that unless you change and become like children, you will never enter the kingdom of heaven. Whoever welcomes a child such as this, welcomes me. If anyone should cause these little ones to lose their faith in me, it would be better for them to have a millstone toed around their neck and be drowned in the deep sea! How terrible, that there are things that make people lose their faith.'

God cares about children, all children, not just vulnerable children. The same verse is repeated in Mark 9: 42 and Luke 17: 1-2. Jesus said, 'things are bound to happen to make people fall into sin, but how terrible for those who make them happen!' There are a number of ways that people abuse or neglect children, but sexual acts.

Matthew 18: 6 But whoever causes one of these little ones who believe in me to sin, it would be better for him to have a great milestone fastened around his neck and to be drowned in the depth of the sea.

The church of Satan in a newspaper article in Newsweek by Nicole Goodkind, dated 14 November 2017, stated regarding Catholic priest paedophiles, 'Christians love pedophilia, as they have been practicing it for years!' They further quote Numbers 31-1-18, Deuteronomy 20:10-14, Judges 21:7-11, Judges 21: 7-10 as bible verses supporting pedophilia and <u>no</u> bible verses condemning it. They say Christians are to blame for pedophilia, but take no responsibility for the demonic influence placed on Christians.

God is not silent on his views of sexual crimes.

13.2 Biblical reference to education, spiritual growth and transformation and emotional development, taboos and teaching.

EDUCATION

Proverbs 22:6

Train up a child in the way he should go, even when he is old he will not depart from it.

Children are a gift from God, while this proverb is a promise from God, some regard it as a warning, but everyone would be wise to recognise the godly principle on which this wisdom is founded.

Every child should be given the opportunity of proper education, training, responsibility, vocation and encouragement, rooted in the word of God, for right living. Although they may stray and become rebellious, there is always hope that the prodigal will return, based on what they learn.

SPIRITUAL GROWTH & TRANSFORMATION

2 Thessalonians 3:13

And as for you, my brothers, and sisters never tire of doing good. In the second letter Paul wrote to the believers at Thessalonica, he gave excellent instructions on spiritual growth. It was to train them in righteousness, mature them in faith, put them back on the spiritual path and to arrest their carnality, yet he made it clear that he did not speak to condemn them, but to assist them.

By advising the Thessalonians that while certain things are permissible, not all things are profitable for spiritual growth or well-being and t warn them not to cause others to stumble in their walk with God. Paul was showing us that it is not possible to save or sanctify ourselves, nor to establish ourselves, but only through the grace of God and the wisdom and knowledge that the Holy Spirit imparts, are we saved.

IN UTERO – THE BEGINNING OF OUR EMOTIONAL DEVELOPMENT

Psalm 139: 13-6 & Luke 1: 41-42, 44

Before the moment of conception, God is aware of us, he knew us before he knit us in our mother's womb. And while we were hiding inside the sheltered womb, no part of us was hidden from God. Our days are ordained by God, before we live even one of them.

When Elizabeth heard Mary's greeting, the baby leaped in her womb and Elizabeth was filled with the Holy Spirit. Elizabeth told Mary, 'Blessed are you among women and blessed is the baby you bear! As soon as your greeting reached my ears, the baby in my womb leaped for joy.

A child in the womb, has been known to interact with other siblings and respond to music. With twins, if one baby is born and one dies prior to being born, or if previous abortions took place in the womb, or miscarriages, there is a 'spirit of death' attached to the womb that oppresses the child through life, unless cut off through spiritual warfare prayer.

Direct impact on an unborn child, comes from the mother, regarding thoughts and feelings. However, it is also important to note that the mother's thoughts and feelings are directly impacted by the father's thoughts and feelings towards the pregnancy. Both parents play an important role in the emotional development of the child, while still in the womb. When rejection is felt, the mother will usually have prolonged labour, or even breach conditions, as the baby feels unwelcome to make their way into the world. Occult rituals or curses spoken over a child in the womb, can open the door to demonic depression and a family history of false spirituality such as Freemasonry, can open the door for oppression or death wishes. [113]

God wants to restore us to his identity and his original intention for us, he is our True Father. Jesus went to the cross, not only to save us from sins or eternal separation from God, but also to redeem our families from curses inherited through our bloodline. It is time to claim our lost inheritance as Jesus sets the captives free.

SEXUAL SIN / SOUL TIES

1 Corinthians 6: 18

Flee from sexual immorality, every other sin a person commits is outside the body, but the sexually immoral person sins against his own body. In the Greco-Roman idol worshipping culture of Paul's day, all forms of sex had been normalised, including prostitution, homosexuality, adultery and so forth. Sex outside of marriage was no longer viewed as a big deal.

---

[113] Healing the past, releasing the future, book by Frank and Catherine Fabiano © 2013, Pages 25-40.

Paul's writings indicated why sexual immorality is essential for believers and why they need to run from it as if from something that will harm them.

Paul shows that sexual immorality differs from other sin, as it unifies them sinfully with those they sin with or against, including pornography. Through this sin, they will experience natural consequences of that sin on that deep level. Sexual immorality contributes to their own deep pain, as opposed to using their bodies to bring glory to God.

13.3 Biblical reference to fatherlessness, mentorship, justice, and the responsibility of the church and teaching.

FATHERLESSNESS

Deuteronomy10:18

He defends the cause of the fatherless and the widow and loves the alien, giving him food and clothing. There are many who do not have the benefit of a father in the home, often causing wrongful behaviour patterns. Mothers nurture, fathers establish identity. Some who have fathers, have encouraged their sons to become criminals and gangsters. Others have fathers who have sexually abused them, or sold them into slavery of child marriage. These fathers aid in the distortion of view that children obtain of God as Father.

Absent fathers have a negative effect on children and the risk of those children developing behavioural problems, joining gangs, turning to drugs and alcohol to numb the pain, or being promiscuous to fill the void, as well as becoming incarcerated, is very high.

We need to share the good news of Jesus Christ to these children and assist them in knowing God as their true Father and that he stands in the gap for the absent father.

MENTORSHIP

Proverbs 27:17

In this fatherless generation, mentors are sorely needed. Mentoring illustrates two important aspects, friendship and accountability. In the Old Testament times, iron blades were used to sharpen other iron blades, in order for them to become more effective tools. This principle can become personal and useful in life, as when two iron blades are left alone, they become blunt and are quite useless. In the same way, God expects us to serve one another and live in a community of believers, building loving relationships and good character. Accountability allows a mentor to look closely into the life of the mentee, so they can see and assist with weaknesses or problem areas.

God can also use the wounds of mentors, to provide healing and motivation to the mentee. At the end of the mentoring, the mentee must look more like Jesus, not the mentor.

JUSTICE / INEQUALITY

Psalm 82:3

Learn to do good, seek justice, correct oppression, bring justice to the fatherless and please the widow's cause. Those who show mercy to others and speak up for the less fortunate, brining equality and fairness, God is delighted in. Those who walk in oppression and labour under discouragement, can take courage that God will be a light to them.

MATTHEW 25:40 / RESPONSIBILITY OF THE CHURCH

Matthew 25:36

I needed clothes and you clothed me, I was sick and you looked after me, I was in prison and you came to visit me. Good works done for Christ's sake mark the character of believers as an effect of grace.

TEACHING

Luke 6:40

The student is not above the teacher, but everyone who is fully trained will be like the teacher.

Jesus was the greatest teacher. Teachers can make or break a student's life. Teachers are often the most selfless, caring and giving individuals in the world. Their aim to see students succeed makes many students thank them for where they are today, in their careers, personal lives and education levels. Offenders mostly come from fatherless, broken homes where no form of encouragement or discipline was administered in their lives. Many of them had absent fathers and mothers who tongue lashed them, telling them they will never amount to anything, 'just like their father.'

Teachers encouraging and believing in students in their personal lives as much as in their educational results, can redirect the student's focus to still be positive. Teachers or volunteers in prisons, make a huge impact in the lives of offenders, relying on God to help reduce recidivism, educate the offender to better his chance of being employed, to direct them to know God personally and to stand in the gap as mentors until they fully rely on God as their true Father. Christian education teachers share morals and values and truths of scripture, as well as model Christian principles and integrity.

Chapter 14 PROGRAM OUTLINES DESIGNED, SPECIFICALLY TAILORED TO NECROPHILIA AND PEDOPHILIA

On conducting research, I browsed the SAQA Unit Standards website to find a measurement tool for programs for sexual offenders, necrophilia, pedophilia and sexual crime. Sadly, none of these items were listed,[114] which indicates the dire need for these interventions to be put in place.

There is a fine line between being a sex addict and a sex offender.

The six essential stages of curriculum development:

- Identify the issue or problem (what problem needs a solution?)
- Characteristics and needs of the participants (who is the target audience?)
- Intended outcomes (what will they be able to do?)
- Content (what material is relevant?)
- Methodology (how will the intended outcomes be achieved?)
- Evaluation strategy and assessment (What works, what measurements qualify?)

---

[114] https://www.saqa.org.za/index.php/search/node?keys= (South African Qualifications Authority (SAQA) Unit Standards Website)

Below please find a basic outline of a Christian based educational program that could be designed for prisons to assist perpetrators of peculiar sexual offences such as: pedophilia and necrophilia:

14.1 Program Name: COMBATTING ATYPICAL SEXUAL MISCONDUCT

Overcoming the compulsions to hunt, torture, rape and kill! The aim of this healing program is to live a non-compulsive, non-secretive and non-shaming sex life.

Dedication

Dedication page with acknowledgements and thanks

About the Author

Short bio of Author achievements, other books published, names of prominent people the program is endorsed by.

Introduction:

'What you feed your mind, transforms your life for better or for worse. What you feed will live, what you starve, will die.'[115]

This program is aimed at assisting perpetrators of necrophilia and pedophilia.

---

[115] Face to face interview, Andrew May, Director Hope Prison Ministry, 7 April 2021.

Many perpetrators seek help, but only find condemnation instead. God longs to heal and restore.

The program consists of 30 classes, includes group counselling as well as homework assignments to be conducted in their cell. One lesson per week to be conducted and one on one counselling can take place after the completion of the entire program, if need be.

Guidelines:

Each lesson should commence and end with prayer and reading of relevant bible verses for the lesson of the day, brought without condemnation, but for purposes of deliverance and freedom within. Most lessons can contain an ice-breaker, to promote ease of conversation and feelings of group inclusion.

This Psychoeducational program[116] should be run by qualified pastors or individuals who are experts on the subject matter as well as involving guest speakers (subject specialists or victim's testimonies) for greater impact. The guidelines will also include specific workshop information, as well as prison rules and information that needs to be adhered to.

Each lesson should comprise of group discussions for counselling therapy, no one should be forced to speak, but rather gently encouraged.

---

[116] Psychoeducational Groups, Description of Support Groups, Book by Nina W. Brown, Page 242.

The paradox of similarity of group members, with similar conditions will grant rationale for the group as a whole.

While offenders may attend this program just for the certificate, for early release, they may be surprised during the program with the work of the Holy Spirit healing them and by the time they give their testimonies, their behaviour and attitude may be completely changed.

Homework should be handed in and each participant should have a book to paste their homework in. Because of the nature of their crimes and for their own safety back in the prison cells, the homework is of a sensitive nature so the offender needs to have their private thoughts protected from other offenders. It is strongly recommended that their homework should be kept by the facilitator until the end of the program, as it will form part of the assessment for their certificate.

Notes to participants / offenders

- This group should be your 'safe place' environment, where you should be able to speak freely about your hurts and share your testimony to encourage others.
- CONFIDENTIALITY is of utmost importance. Please do not share anything you hear inside the group, outside the group. We cannot guarantee that everyone will follow this guideline, thus please be cautious with what you share.

- If a participant decides to share information that constitutes illegal activities, the group enabler may not contact the authorities without your permission.
- Please be sensitive to the needs of others, try not to dominate the conversation while another person is sharing.
- The group offers group counselling during the workshop, however one-on-one counselling can be arranged for deeper and more private issues.
- Be prepared to hear 'that does not apply to me' however adapt the information to your own struggles and remain teachable.
- Healing takes time and I understand that I need to trust God with the process.
- While 'Combatting Atypical Sexual Misconduct' offers support, only Jesus is the true healer!
- The aim of this healing program is to live a non-compulsive, non-secretive and non-shaming sex life and living a life of freedom and integrity.
- Just being in prison is NOT going to correct you.

Confidentiality

Confidentiality must be respected at all times, for all participants and even among facilitators.

Specific outcomes

Measurement of program against SAQA unit standards, other comparisons with specific outcomes tailored to necrophilia and pedophilia.

Table of Contents (see below)

Table of contents outlined, including homework which counts towards assessments for certificates.

12 Steps of Sex Addict Recovery Declarations

To be spoken out loud in the group daily:

Step 1	I admit that I are powerless over addictive sexual behaviour, that my life has become unmanageable
Step 2	I believe that God can heal me and he will never give up on me
Step 3	I have made a decision to turn my life around and give my will over to God, so that his will can be done
Step 4	With God's help, I will make a soul searching and fearless moral inventory of my life
Step 5	I will admit to God, to myself and to others, the exact nature of my crimes and wrongdoing
Step 6	I am surrendering my whole self to God, to remove these defects of my character

Step 7	I humbly ask God to forgive me, strengthen my resolve, heal my thought patterns and wrong desires and to remove my shortcomings
Step 8	I will make a list of all the people I have harmed and become willing to make amends with them
Step 9	I will pray for God to help the victims that I have caused harm to, to be healed and to forgive me
Step 10	I will take full responsibility for my crimes and put myself in a position where I will be accountable to a mentor, who will walk a road with me and pray for me
Step 11	I will read God's word daily for spiritual growth and inner healing
Step 12	I will trust God with my future and practise these principles to avoid committing sexual crimes and violating others or putting them in harm's way

End Notes

Acknowledgements of research, information sources, pictures and dates of downloading.

Sexual Addiction Self-Screening Quiz – (To be conducted prior to the program)

This simple test is designed to give you clarity, to determine if you are a sex addict. All answers are either Yes / No and do not pertain to current day, but to consider your sexual history as a whole.

1. Do you find that sexual fantasy, having and seeking sex is more important in your life than God and other things?
2. Do you regret the amount of time you waste fantasising about or searching for sex?
3. Have you continually promised yourself that you will stop visiting porn sites?
4. If you are in a committed relationship or marriage, do you find yourself dwindling off at times for secretive sexual affairs or sexually related activities?
5. Do you visit porn websites and waste time in 'losing yourself' for a few hours, when you only intended being on for a few minutes?
6. Has your focus on sex driven you away from your family, friends, church and other important aspects of your life?
7. Do you lie in bed at night and dream about sex with corpses?
8. Do you fantasise about sex with children?
9. Do you fantasise about killing, for sexual gratification?
10. Do you act on any of your fantasies or committed an illegal crime because of your sexual desires?

11. Has your sexual activities ever caused you deep losses, of family, jobs, money, status, God, etc.?
12. Do you cover up certain sexual behaviour patterns for fear of being caught?
13. Does your wife/partner know everything about you sexual activities?
14. Have you ever been arrested or reprimanded for sexually related charges?
15. Do you engage in drugs or/and alcohol?
16. Do you download pornographic material and hide it?
17. Have you ever exploited children in a sexually related manner?
18. Do you become ashamed, angry or offensive when asked about your sexual activities?
19. Have you ever suffered from sexually transmitted diseases?
20. Have you ever paid for sex?
21. Were you exposed to sexually related things from an early age?
22. Do you desire to change?
23. Do you accept God wants to make the changes and loves you despite any sin you may have committed?
24. Do you desire healing and restoration?
25. Are you ready to make a firm commitment to yourself for freedom from bondage?

If you answered YES to a few questions from 1 - 20, you are at risk of being a sex addict, if you answered YES to most questions there is a definite possibility you are a sex addict.

If you answered YES to question 9, you need to seek wise counsel and professional advice.

14.2 PART I - PEDOPHILIA

Understanding victim responses to pedophilia abuse

Most victims of pedophilia, start cutting themselves, as the pain they inflict on themselves is more acceptable than the pain that was inflicted on them, by their perpetrators. Some victims also turn to alcohol, drugs, fire setting, social isolation, pornography, sexual promiscuity, paraphilia, violence or abuse of animals, as a way of expressing their inner hurt.

A paedophiles poem:

A poem written that depicts a warning; and anguish the victim of paedophile feels: Quoted from ~ https://allpoetry.com/poems/about/Pedophilia.

Monsters Lurking Around

A young girl's mind played with and destroyed
they hurt me so bad with the tricks they deployed.
Words and sweet talk, behaviours so low
if I told you about them your mind would blow.
How can someone be so cruel?
How can someone hurt a child?
Play games like that
It's just wild.
They made up lies,
Playing with my innocent heart.
I think being a paedophile is some twisted art.
No can't call it an art,
That's an insult to artists.
These perpetrators are just completely heartless.
They are the monsters inside your closet
except they walk free in the open.
The funny thing is... everyone knows them.
They are so good at what they do
their moves will for sure fool you.
Watch out for the monsters that are lurking around
You may think you know none
but they are everywhere to be found.[117]

---

[117] https://allpoetry.com/poems/about/Pedophilia

Table of Contents

Ice-Breaker

Fun ice-breakers help participants relax and laughter bonds people.

Pre-Lesson   Identifying My Pedophilia Selection

Infantophilia	Babies 0-3 years old
Pedophilia	Children aged 5-10 years old
Hebephiliac	Children aged 11-16 years old
Paedo-Sadism	Torturing of children *Dark web

Lesson 1   Understanding the dark abyss of pedophilia

Explanation of pedophilia and its ripple effects on victims, family members, community members. Two victims can be invited to give a testimony of how pedophilia affected their lives detrimentally, yet God restored them. Paedophiles to discuss how they feel misunderstood, judged and ridiculed. Many come from disengaged and rigid families. Paedophiles may have more than one addiction and a history of criminogenic thinking of hunt, torture, rape and kill.[118]

Homework:

Read the poem and write down your feelings or own poem about how you felt when you attended the first class.

---

[118] Mending a shattered heart book, Stefanie Carnes, Pages 133-134

Lesson 2   Overcoming rejection from childhood

Dealing with rejection from parents, siblings, friends, school teachers, school bullies, relatives who abandoned, God will never leave you nor abandon you. Discussions on when the feelings of pedophilia started. Father-Hunters, father hungry young men seeking older men for sex, due to seeking male attention they lacked from their father.[119]

Homework:

Write a letter to your victims or family members that were hurt by your actions and how you feel about it.

Lesson 3   How do I set boundaries to keep myself and children safe from my pedophilia condition? Understanding the child's need for safety and protection from early sexual experiences.

We cannot bandage the wounds of victims beneath the wheels of injustice, but need to drive a spike into the wheel itself. Boundaries can be confining, yet freeing. Healthy boundaries need to be established as a crucial part of healing and functioning in future. It takes practise to identify and set boundaries as well as pace your responses to negative impulses and change your mind-set. Children should not be exposed to sex too early, as it has major detrimental effects on their psyche, they need to be

---

[119] Mending a shattered heart book, Stefanie Carnes, Pages 165-166

protected. How will I stop using the teddy bear symbol to signify my pedophilia to other paedophiles?

Homework:

Write a letter to a child called 'John or Jill' apologising for your actions and how you regret what you have done to them. List ways you have tried to quit or curtail your sexual behaviours.

Lesson 4   Letting go of anger

Anger from childhood leads to making many wrong life choices and decisions. An angry man who feels he has nothing to lose, is a very dangerous thing. Identifying narcissists. What triggers anger and how can we just let it go?

Homework:

Write a two page essay on what triggers your anger, what things are you angry about since childhood, who are you angry with and why, how have you been wronged and how you think God can help you to overcome the past?

Lesson 5   Guilt, Shame and Blame

An offence always creates a debt. One of Satan's most strategic methods of keeping us back from being healed and having a loving relationship with God the father, is by holding us hostage in a place of guilt, shame and blame, as well as using sex as a way of humiliating and shaming.

Four dimensions of guilt will be discussed: Supressed guilt, acknowledged guilt, false guilt and no guilt.

Homework:

Draw a picture or write a paragraph of how you see God. Is he loving, angry, fearsome or distant? Write down a bible verse that describes God as a loving God.

Lesson 6   Managing Sex and other addictions and attractions

'The eyes are not responsible, when the mind does the seeing.' ~David Klatzow.[120]

Manging the sex addiction is a daily struggle, when pornographic images torment the mind and sexual urges overshadow reasoning. There are many pornographic traps, including the dark web. Write down your triggers.

Homework:

Write a letter to God asking him to forgive you and help free you and protect your mind from previous pornographic images that torment you. Spend more time reading the bible and praying and eventually the images will fade and God will create new beautiful images and

---

[120] Justice Denied, book by David Klatzow, The fickle fingers of fate, Page 46.

thoughts. Ask God to renew your mind and help you put on the mind of Christ.

Lesson 7 Bad sex verses good sex, as God designed it

God designed sex as a beautiful act between marriage partners, husbands and wives, but the devil distorts it. Overcoming temptations and desires of the sinful nature.

Homework:

Write an essay on how you think relationships work, as God designed them.

Lesson 8 Embracing self-esteem that God gives

Learn to embrace a healthy self-esteem that God gives, not a false love and self-esteem that is derived from lust and sex, in a way that is not intended by God. Family structure and background and lack of love, affects self-esteem.[121]

Homework:

Write a letter to your younger self, advising yourself of the glorious future God has in store for you, embracing a healthy self-esteem, as you are made in his image.

Lesson 9 Forgiveness of parents and others

The domineering mother, the absent or abusive father, the teacher who ridiculed, the children who bullied, the best

---

[121] Come Clean Book, by Doug Herman, Page 26.

friend who betrayed. Forgiveness is the turning point to healing.[122]

Homework:

Write a letter to God, telling him who you choose to forgive and why.

Lesson 10   Demonic influence deliverance

A forgiveness and deliverance session, to be run by someone trained in proper demonic deliverance. Letting go of the inner demons, to embrace the new life God sets before you. Ensure the participants are prayed over, anointed with oil and filled with the Holy Spirit before leaving the class. Shedding the 'entitlement and victim' mentality.

Homework:

Write down your concerns and anxieties for how you feel you will be treated when released from prison and how you can start to build and establish support structures and coping mechanisms.

Lesson 11   Coping outside of prison

Coping mechanisms and skills for outside of prison, knowing the community of not very forgiving or accepting of paedophiles and slowly showing them you have

---

[122] Come Clean Book, by Doug Herman, Page 75-76.

transformed through the help of Jesus Christ. How to cope with suffering and in so, knowing God is in control.

Homework:

Reflection on the entire course and preparation of your testimony of what this course has meant to you. Do you feel changed, or changes are in slow progress, or did the course have no effect on you at all? Do you feel fear or optimism? How to know God's will for your life.

Lesson 13   Gender based violence - men abusing children, women abusing children

Life skills, social skills, spiritual growth and formation skills, laws against pedophilia, crushing the excuse for abuse. An ounce of prevention is worth more than a pound of cure.

Lesson 14   Case Studies – Group Discussions and Therapy

Group to be split in two, discuss two specific case studies of pedophilia and have a qualified person round the session off with sound advice. Session to be interactive so that the perpetrator does not feel condemned or judged, but rather understood and cared for by God.

Homework:

Write an essay on what you learned from the case studies.

Lesson 15   Defining healthy sexual relationships

Self-nurturing, relationships, appropriate environments, the right people, sex the way God designed it.

Homework:

Write an essay on how you will define and establish healthy sexual relationships in the future.

Lesson 16   How to grow spiritually

To grow spiritually, means to become more like the Lord Jesus in the way we live. Not just to gain knowledge, but to act on what we learn, so that what we learn, transforms us. God is responsible for changing our character, we are responsible for changing our behaviour.

Homework:

Write an essay on how you have transformed spiritually during this program.

Conclusion

A motivational talk to be conducted by the facilitator on the following topic: '*From the day we were born, we were given a life sentence, how we choose to live it, will determine our liberty or captivity.*'

Assessment

A test designed for participants to complete on what they learned, for a certificate which can be handed out at the closing ceremony. These assessments are marked by facilitators, but can be forwarded to an assessor or moderator, if the offender does not agree with the results.

Pledge

A pledge that each offender writes and signs, based on what they learned in the above lessons. These pledges can be read out as part of their testimony of what this course has meant to them at the closing ceremony. If the participants wish to keep their pledge private, they may do so.

Closing ceremony / testimony session / certification

Handing out of certificates, no one should fail this program unless they had 0% participation, inclusion in group discussions or interest in wanting to change.

At the closing ceremony, each participant to receive a rubber band to put on their arm, with the explanation that when sexual thoughts trigger their minds, they are to within three seconds pull back the rubber band and shoot themselves on the wrist. This action will distracts their thoughts.

14.3 PART II - NECROPHILIA

Understanding the silence of necrophilia - no victims of the crime, to tell the tale

Necrophilia is the silent crime is hardly ever reported, unless the perpetrator is caught red handed or gives himself up. The real victims in this situation are the traumatised living relatives and friends, of the abused corpse.

Fear that drives the perpetrators pleasure

Perpetrators instil fear in their vulnerable victims, which the more they are tortured, fear, scream and seem helpless, the more pleasure is derived by the offender.

A necrophiles poem: (*A poem written by a necrophile, as he sees the corpse): Quoted from:* https://www.poetryinternational.org

Parting kiss

No wayward promise,
Nothing to shake the heart,
Nothing to warm to,
No trace of harm or hurt,
Nothing of jealousy,
No risk of bliss,
The wide, white eye,
The perfect parting kiss.[123]

---

[123] https://www.poetryinternational.org/pi/poem/ 11676/auto/0/0/David-Harsent/ Necrophilia/en/tile

Table of Contents

Ice-Breaker

Fun ice-breakers help participants relax and laughter bonds people.

Pre-Lesson   Identifying My Necrophilia Selection

Role Player
Vampire
Cannibal *Eating
Sentimental
Fantasizer
Material *Tongue
Fetishistic
Necromutilo Maniac *Dismembering
Sharp *Shroud
Maniacal *Murder
Restrictive * Intercourse

Lesson 1   Understanding the dark passages of necrophilia

Explanation of necrophilia and its ripple effects on victims, family members, community members. Two criminologists can be invited to give a testimony of how necrophilia affected people's lives detrimentally, yet God restored them. Necrophiles to discuss how they feel misunderstood, judged and ridiculed.

Many come from disengaged and rigid families. Necrophiles may have more than one addiction and a history of criminogenic thinking criminogenic thinking of hunt, torture, rape and kill.

Homework:

Read the poem and write down your feelings or own poem about how you felt when you attended the first class.

Lesson 2   Overcoming rejection from childhood

Dealing with rejection from parents, siblings, friends, school teachers, school bullies, relatives who abandoned, God will never leave you nor abandon you. The domineering mother, the absent or abusive father, the teacher who ridiculed, the children who bullied, the best friend who betrayed. Discussions on when the feelings of necrophilia started. Father-Hunters, father hungry young men seeking older men for sex, due to seeking male attention they lacked from their father.

Homework:

Write a letter to your victims or family members that were hurt by your actions and how you feel about it.

Lesson 3   How do I set boundaries to keep myself safe from temptations and jobs when I am near corpses or have the urge to kill? Understanding the

victim's right to life, need for safety and protection.

We cannot bandage the wounds of victims beneath the wheels of injustice, but need to drive a spike into the wheel itself. Boundaries can be confining, yet freeing. Healthy boundaries need to be established as a crucial part of healing and functioning in future. It takes practise to identify and set boundaries as well as pace your responses to negative impulses and change your mind-set. Corpses should not be violated and disrespected, as it has major detrimental effects on the living family members when they find out. List ways you have tried to quit or curtail your sexual behaviours.

Homework:

Write a letter to a corpse called 'John or Jill' apologising for your actions and how you regret what you have done to them, as well as their living relatives.

Lesson 4   Letting go of anger

Anger from childhood leads to making many wrong life choices and decisions. An angry man who feels he has nothing to lose, is a very dangerous thing. Identifying narcissists. What triggers anger and how can we just let it go?

Homework:

Write a two page essay on what triggers your anger, what things are you angry about since childhood, who are you angry with and why, how have you been wronged and how you think God can help you to overcome the past?

Lesson 5   Guilt, Shame and Blame

One of Satan's most strategic methods of keeping us back from being healed and having a loving relationship with God the father, is by holding us hostage in a place of guilt, shame and blame, as well as using sex as a way of humiliating and shaming.

Homework:

Draw a picture or write a paragraph of how you see God. Is he loving, angry, fearsome or distant? Write down a bible verse that describes God as a loving God.

Lesson 6   Managing Sex and other addictions and attractions

'The eyes are not responsible, when the mind does the seeing.' ~David Klatzow.

Manging the sex addiction is a daily struggle, when pornographic images torment the mind and sexual urges overshadow reasoning. There are many pornographic traps, including the dark web. Write down your triggers.

Homework:

Write a letter to God asking him to forgive you and help free you and protect your mind from previous pornographic images that torment you. Spend more time reading the bible and praying and eventually the images will fade and God will create new beautiful images and thoughts. Ask God to renew your mind and help you put on the mind of Christ.

Lesson 7   Bad sex verses good sex, as God designed it

God designed sex as a beautiful act between marriage partners, husbands and wives, but the devil distorts it. Overcoming temptations and desires of the sinful nature.

Homework:

Write an essay on how you think relationships work, as God designed them.

Lesson 8   Embracing self-esteem that God gives

Learn to embrace a healthy self-esteem that God gives, not a false love and self-esteem that is derived from lust and sex, in a way that is not intended by God.

Homework:

Write a letter to your younger self, advising yourself of the glorious future God has in store for you, embracing a healthy self-esteem, as you are made in his image.

Lesson 9   Understanding decomposition of corpses and the diseases they carry

Having decomposition of corpses explained, to a degree of making the perpetrator realising the health risks and abnormality of the attraction to them. Teaching them integrity, respect and accountability, including respecting a corpse and giving it a proper burial as God would intend, as nothing is hidden from his sight.

Homework:

Write a paragraph about what integrity, respect and accountability means to you.

Lesson 10   Forgiveness of parents and others

The domineering mother, the absent or abusive father, the teacher who ridiculed, the children who bullied, the best friend who betrayed. Forgiveness is the turning point to healing.

Homework:

Write a letter to God, telling him who you choose to forgive and why.

Lesson 11   Demonic influence deliverance

A forgiveness and deliverance session, to be run by someone trained in proper demonic deliverance. Letting go of the inner demons, to embrace the new life God sets before you. Ensure the participants are prayed over, anointed with oil and filled with the Holy Spirit before leaving the class. How to cope with suffering and in so, knowing God is in control.

Homework:

Write down your concerns and anxieties for how you feel you will be treated when released from prison and how you can start to build and establish support structures and coping mechanisms.

Lesson 12   Coping outside of prison

Coping mechanisms and skills for outside of prison, knowing the community of not very forgiving or accepting of paedophiles and slowly showing them you have transformed through the help of Jesus Christ. How to know God's will for your life.

Homework:

Reflection on the entire course and preparation of your testimony of what this course has meant to you. Do you feel changed, or changes are in slow progress, or did the course have no effect on you at all? Do you feel fear or optimism?

Lesson 13   Gender based violence - men abusing women abusing women, women abusing men, same sex abusing same sex, people abusing corpses, how people should treat and respect each other

Life skills, social skills, spiritual growth and formation skills, laws against necrophilia, crushing the excuse for abuse. An ounce of prevention is worth more than a pound of cure.

Lesson 14   Case Studies – Group Discussions and Therapy

Group to be split in two, discuss two specific case studies of necrophilia and have a qualified person round the session off with sound advice. Session to be interactive so that the perpetrator does not feel condemned or judged, but rather understood and cared for by God.

Homework:

Write an essay on what you learned from the case studies.

Lesson 15   Defining healthy sexual relationships

Self-nurturing, relationships, appropriate environments, the right people, sex the way God designed it.

Homework:

Write an essay on how you will define and establish healthy sexual relationships in the future.

Lesson 16   How to grow spiritually

To grow spiritually, means to become more like the Lord Jesus in the way we live. Not just to gain knowledge, but to act on what we learn, so that what we learn, transforms us. God is responsible for changing our character, we are responsible for changing our behaviour.

Homework:

Write an essay on how you have transformed spiritually during this program.

Conclusion

A motivational talk to be conducted by the facilitator on the following topic: '*From the day we were born, we were given a life sentence, how we choose to live it, will determine our liberty or captivity.*'

Assessment

A test designed for participants to complete on what they learned, for a certificate which can be handed out at the closing ceremony. These assessments are marked by facilitators, but can be forwarded to an assessor or moderator, if the offender does not agree with the results.

Pledge

A pledge that each offender writes and signs, based on what they learned in the above lessons. These pledges can be read out as part of their testimony of what this course has meant to them at the closing ceremony. If the participants wish to keep their pledge private, they may do so.

Closing ceremony / testimony session / certification.

Handing out of certificates, no one should fail this program unless they had 0% participation, inclusion in group discussions or interest in wanting to change.

At the closing ceremony, each participant to receive a rubber band to put on their arm, with the explanation that when sexual thoughts trigger their minds, they are to within three seconds pull back the rubber band and shoot themselves on the wrist. This action will distracts their thoughts.

14.4 Counselling with a Social Justice Perspective

Many paedophiles and necrophiles are narcissist, yet some who seek healing are too embarrassed and feel shame to admit their actions and fantasies. They may enjoy having a secret and never telling anyone, for reasons which include protecting their family, or to avoid being beaten up, being ostracised or going to prison, being thrown out of their community or losing their jobs or statuses.

With Christian education run in prisons, counselling is significant and in most cases, essential. Counselling can be conducted in two manners:

Group Counselling:

Christian group counselling is most effective through a church where healing and love embraces all, where there is acceptance of dissent and difference where conformity gives way to the spirit of freedom.

Counselling and support groups are advisable to help reduce emotional pain and anguish experienced by perpetrators and victims, for healing for all kinds of traumatic events. Stemming from what transpires during group counselling, certain individuals would need one-on-one further counselling.

Jesus is pictured as a great small group counsellor in history, our perfect model to follow. Jesus' involvement with small groups is the most convincing rationale for why churches need to include them in their congregational lives. Jesus started off by gathering his twelve disciples, taught and counselled them, met up with them constantly, shared meals, encouraged one another (edification), ministered together (intentional gathering), experienced hardship together and strengthened their relationships with one another (fellowship). Jesus' goal was to equip the small group to develop them to continue his ministry after he left.

The Holy Spirit must be a group member in order for the counselling to be effective. The way the Holy Spirit performs in the counselling group is through eight methods:

The Revealer	Reveals the root of the problem
The Indweller	Present in every meeting
The Enabler	Source of our spiritual gifts and gives us the ability to serve one another
The Convictor	Bears witness and convicts us of wrong attitudes and actions
The Intercessor	Intercedes with God the Father on our behalf, helps us in our spiritual weakness
The Teacher	Reminds us of God's word, teaches us through illumination of biblical text and helps us understand biblical truth

The Unifier	As God's people we are one, spiritual unity in a group is possible
The Guide	Provides guidance, whether making decisions, choosing scripture, rejoicing over someone's healing and success. We must remain sensitive

The group leader must be in a personal relationship with God, have commitment to caring for people, desire to serve, willingness to learn, be trustworthy and confidential, be a good listener and advisor, be focused with vision and purpose, deal with conflict effectively, understand effective communication, in some cases be a subject matter expert and have a formal facilitator qualification and an understanding of spiritual principles.

One-on-One Counselling:

During conducting the above program in which group counselling has taken place, one-on-one counselling should follow, for those offenders with deeper psychological issues and need for inner healing.

Respectful counselling framework includes considerations in factors such as economic class background, criminal background, length of sentencing, possibility or non-possibility of parole, sentence being served for specific crime, family background and history, cultural background, age, gender, spiritual maturity, stress levels, educational level, mental health and state of mind, emotional edge, language barriers, past trauma, medical condition, suicide tendencies, difficulty in transitioning or adjusting to prison life, prison rules and limitations and offender support systems from outside prison.

Christian Counselling should always include giving homework to the offender, to work though, which comprises of bible verses, reading materials, depending on literacy level ability. An offender will often approach a counsellor or social worker, to request that they counsel someone on the outside of prison, a relative or friend they may be concerned about. Counselling an offender with a negative mind-set is a sensitive matter and words of advice should be chosen carefully.

The Holy Spirit must be a present during counselling, in order for the session to be effective.

The difference between group and individual counselling:

The distinguished difference between group and individual counselling gives the benefit of comfort, for those who are struggling to realise that they are not alone. This helps normalise the situation and reduce shame and leads to recovery.

Pastoral Care Counselling

Spiritual Care Workers (SCW) in prisons offer the service of Pastoral Care to offenders, which has four important characteristics:

- The SCW must be like Jesus, the good Shepherd
- The SCW must be a loving, caring, people's person
- The SCW must be a person who can be trusted
- The SCW must be a person who has a deep spiritual life, a relationship with God

Offenders, like others, suffer from the following emotional problems that need healing:

- Shock
- Denial
- Anger
- Negotiation
- Mixed feelings
- Depression
- Fear and loneliness
- Acceptance
- Forgiveness
- Trust

For purposes of Pastoral Care, The SCW must make a point of:

- Treating each offender as unique, humane and special in God's eyes
- Take the faith and values of the offender seriously
- Take the expectations of the offender seriously
- Allow the offender to have a voice
- Allow the offender an opportunity for inner emotional healing, to know God
- Be willing to pray for and with the offender
- Be willing to have contact with the offender's family
- Be willing to conduct counselling with the offender, as well as their family members if need be
- Be willing to deal with conflict among offenders, God's way
- Encourage offenders that God gives up on no-one and that with God's help, they can make positive changes in their lives
- Give offenders equal opportunities access to education, secular as well as Christian

Offenders have seven basic needs that need to be met, which the SCW must assist with:

- Safe shelter needs
- Physical needs
- Social needs
- Emotional needs
- Spiritual needs
- Educational needs
- Medical needs

14.5 Perpetrator and victim counselling

Healing programs are to be effectively implemented within pastoral care functions, the skills of the facilitator required will depend on the sexual violence or crime, as well as emotional response. Counselling will only be effective if respect, concreteness, warmth, empathy, genuineness, non-violent confrontation and confidentiality is applied (Lartey 2003: 89-101).

According to (Adams 1994:59), 'A pastor, minister or counsellor's role is to assist victims and perpetrators to understand the significance of a coordinated community response as the only way to truly protect and call, to accountability.'

The need for counselling that combines Christian education, needs to replace the traditional model of pastoral care, with a new approach:

Traditional Model	Proactive Model
Pedophilia viewed as a male issue	Pedophilia viewed as non-gender issue
Necrophilia viewed as 'peculiar and untreatable'	Affirming that with God, change is possible
Dematerialising the crisis by being focused on religious issues	Focus on physical and spiritual trauma and healing
Getting perpetrators and victims to talk about their problems	Implement professional referrals, shelters, psychologists, criminal justice systems
Assume or accept the perpetrator is mentally ill or born that way	Accountability and responsibility for behaviour patterns

Counsellor or pastoral care to consider these questions, in counselling:

- Do I understand the life threatening nature and control the perpetrator has over the victim?
- Do I understand the confidentiality required, to keep the victim or perpetrator safe?
- Do I understand the victim's version of what happened, correctly? Does it differ as the questioning evolves?
- Am I prepared to challenge the differences?
- How do I identify the root of the problem and am I equipped enough to deal with it?

- Do I have reliable a referral system in place, to assist the counselee?
- Since I represent the church, as the umbrella under which I counsel, am I objective and non-judgemental in my response to answers I receive, to my questions?

All people in a position to teach adult or child Christian education need to be registered with South African Council for Educators (SACE) counsel and need to undergo the necessary, professional training and when counselling, belong to a professional counselling governing body, Association of Christian Religious Practitioners, or Association of Registered Councillors South Africa (ARCSA). Coupled with that, the necessary education and qualification to deal with the specialised need, child counselling, pedophilia, necrophilia.

14.6 Restorative justice for victims

What is restorative justice?

Restorative justice is a generic term for wrongdoing that seeks to move beyond condemnation, punishment or seeking justice, or amnesty, in a manner of making peace between the offender and victim, community members or family groups, promoting accountability and forgiveness.

Restorative justice provides for a 'safe space' for all parties to reconcile in a controlled environment, restore relationships and resolve conflict, with dignity.

Restorative justice educational program processes, give expression to values, respect, honesty, humility, trust, accountability in a just process that allows all parties to have ample opportunity and listen, managed by a mediator.

Empowerment

Crime robs victims of their power, since other people exert control over them, without their consent. Restorative justice seeks to empower victims by giving them an active role in determining their needs and how they should be met. It also empowers offenders to take personal responsibility and accountability for the offence and what they can do to remedy the harm they have done, to rehabilitate and restore the relationship by apologizing and explaining, while the mediator considers all preceding factors from all parties present.

No matter how severe the wrongdoing, it is always possible for the victims that are suffering, to respond in love, forgiveness, hope and strength which promotes positive healing and change. Restorative justice does not seek to punish past behaviour, but to address it and bring hope for the future, a positive outcome for all, albeit a painful process.

Mediators and the 'having a voice' process

Restorative justice is not an alternative to the criminal law system, the law always takes first place, but educates offenders and victims on reconciliation.

Mediators should always be objective and remain neutral. The mediator manages the process and the students should agree and deliver on them, in a disciplined, values-based manner. The process should be open to all students in a fair manner that allows all present, to speak about their feelings and opinions in a way that resolves the problem, benefitting all. The process provides information, rather than determining the outcome. No one should feel forced or coerced to remain in the process, staying in it should be voluntary. All mediation should be kept confidential and all parties shown due respect, throughout the process.

The process should validate the victim's experience, feelings, losses, hurt and questions, without reproach or criticism or judgement on the part of the offender. The offender in turn, is not obligated to tell all, but it would help the outcomes, promote healing and closure and stimulate the relationship to be restored and healthier.

It is important that all who have a voice, have the opportunity to be heard.

Core values in the restorative justice system

Core values assist the advancement of justice in the wider community, family groups, offenders and victim relationships and the effects of the crimes and repairing harm within these structures. The primary core value is mutual respect.

Healing process

Not all restorative justice cases are solved with satisfactory outcomes for all parties, but the goal is to find common ground, where healing can begin. If blame is continually placed on each other, no one will find answers or heal, in fact it could evoke anger and bitterness, instead of forgiveness and healing.

Many family members who have experienced a family member being murdered for example, just want answers as to what happened, how did they die, what was their last words, where the body was buried or hidden, who else was involved, was their death painful? In the case of missing relatives, were they abducted, were they killed, will they ever see them again and will the victim ever come home? Restorative justice with the offender resolves a few of these issues, but only if the offender is honest and tells the whole truth. Once the victims know, they can choose to forgive and start healing emotionally, spiritually and sometimes physically.

The healing process may bring the offender amnesty, or in some cases lighter sentencing, but will still be held accountable by law.

The advantages of restorative justice educational processes are first and foremost in bringing home to the offender the consequences of his wrongdoing and making him accountable, while meeting the needs of the victims so that they are no longer victims. Restorative justice restores peace from terrible things that have happened.

The day Jesus died, he revealed the meaning of true justice. Justice is not a form of revenge, but purely of forgiveness.

Chapter 15   CONCLUSION / HYPO BOOKS

God's perfect grace, mercy and forgiveness extends to serial killers, stalkers, abusers, murders, paedophiles, necrophiles, sadists, bullies, robbers, sex offenders, thieves, Satanists, gamblers, rebels, gangsters, mentally ill related crimes and war crime perpetrators. We have all sinned and fallen short of the glory of God and if life was fair, we would all deserve a prison sentence, but no-one is beyond help and God will certainly not give up on anyone. If we have walked away with someone else's pen, we are a thief. If we have gossiped about someone, the Bible terms us as murderers. But, if people that have committed heinous crimes like pedophilia and necrophilia and ask Jesus to transform their lives, will he show *them* mercy? Or is mercy only reserved for a few?

Sexual arousal, sexual sadism and intimacy aversion are not the fullness of possible explanations as to why individuals engage in necrophilia and pedophilia. The research in this book has shown that behavioural patterns and responses are able to be provided treatment for, as well as getting to the root of the problem.

The sexual arousal mechanism needs to be determined and dealt with. It is to be decided if the other crimes united with necrophilia or pedophilia, may be the broader issue or challenge that needs to be dealt with instead.

It needs to be clarified if the prison sentences imposed are adequate and appropriate, or if alternative methods can be sought, such as secular or Christian educational programs. Prison itself, may not be the answer at all. Based on the study conducted herein, if Christian based programs, specifically tailored to necrophiles and paedophiles can be introduced to the prisons, it will positively impact their lives, however the choice to want to change, always remains the offenders.

Numerous hypo books have been proposed, regarding the cause of this peculiar behaviour. According to Schafer and Krudten (1977: 57) modern biological criminology theory bases its origins in classical and positive schools of thought. The hereditary-theorists base their beliefs on the possibility that criminal genes are passed from generation to generation, however later studies showed that the biological view has been questioned and has no relevance. The psychological theory differs from the biological, as it views deviance as a mental illness, rather than biological inheritance or characteristic. These facts prove it difficult to find solutions, to assist them, as there are no known Christian educational programs utilized in the prisons in South Africa to ease this burden in society.

Do we as society proudly shake our heads at them, in shame, judgement and disgust? Do we believe that the devil has them in his clutches and that's all they deserve?

Or do we truly believe God still loves them, has an abundance of grace for them and is able to heal them? Or should we rather hang our heads in shame, because we shun them and are not brave enough to help them?

The roots of human dignity and international human rights can be traced back to the college envisioned by Calvin which was established in Geneva over 460 years ago. Comprehensive research should continue to similarly unravel the complexity of the vicious cycle of recidivism, reintegration and rehabilitation. Prisons are grossly overcrowded, alternative solutions to prison sentences should be considered, such as compulsory education classes and other recommendations made in Chapter 12 above.

This book has proved that secular accredited education, makes a difference towards employment skills. Christian education builds character and promotes spiritual growth and transformation. According to experts, both educational systems reduce recidivism, however they are more convinced that Christian education, has the greater impact. It also proves that taxpayers are not aware that they do not pay for any education for offenders, beyond R200 annually per offender, that is studying ABET. Taxpayer's monies pay for food and accommodation, not rehabilitation.

More could be done to bridge the gap between offender, family and community.

We can conclude that the church needs to step up and take responsibility to illuminate education as the pursuit of knowledge which is a basic human right and Christian education which will promote spiritual growth and transformation. This model of non-judgmental approach to love and justice is a corrective measure which will focus on reduction of recidivism and rehabilitation.

Perpetrators of necrophilia would perhaps respond that they are doing nothing wrong at all, and that the act or crime is as beautiful as art or poetry itself!

Victims would have a few strong objectives and valid reasoning of possible outcomes, general society may feel less irrepressible.

Educators with the correct training and in a good standing relationship with God, will make a positive impact in changing lives, stopping the detrimental life cycles of recidivism and encourage offenders to stay rooted in Christ Jesus.

Education is key, love is essential and grace is inevitable.

'Education changes people, thus we do not need more prisons, but rather we need more classrooms.' ~Quote Jennifer Lackey, Director of North-western Prison Education Program and Philosophy Professor at North-western University.

BIBLIOGRAPHY / ACKNOWLEDGEMENTS

i. List of Sources: Books, Authors and Publishers:

1. ***Abnormal Psychology,*** *book by David H. Barlow and V. Mark Durand (Published by Wadsworth, Canada) © Fifth Edition 2009.*

2. ***Addressing Barriers to Learning, A South African perspective,*** *book by Author Emmerentia Landsberg (Published by Van Schaik Publishers, Pretoria) © 2005.*

3. ***Advances in Fingerprint Technology,*** *book by C. Lee, R.E. Gaensslen (Published by CRC Press, Boca Raton, London and New York, USA) © Second Edition 2001.*

4. ***An Appraisal of Forensic Science Evidence in Criminal Proceedings,*** *book by Norbert Ebisike (Published by Greenway, San Francisco, USA) © First edition 2001.*

5. ***Basic Education in Prisons,*** *book by UNESCO Institute for Education (Published by Maryland State Department of Education, Austria and Germany) © 1995.*

6. ***Bill of Rights Handbook, Fifth Edition,*** *by Authors Iain Currie & Johan der Waal (Published by Juta, Lansdowne, Cape Town) © 2005.*

7. ***Bridge of Hope, A Counselling Guide for Pastors and Spiritual Workers,*** *book by Piet and Elsabe Oosthuizen (Published by Bible Media, Wellington, South Africa) © First Edition, 1992.*

8. ***Child Pornography and Sexual Grooming: Legal and Societal Responses,*** *by Suzanne Ost (Published by Cambridge University Press, New York, USA) © 2009.*

9. ***Community Counselling, a Multi-cultural Social justice Perspective,*** *book by Judith A. Lewis, Michael D. Lewis, Judy A. Daniels, Michael J. D'Andrea (USA) © Fourth Edition, International Version 2011.*

10. ***Conversations with Myself, Nelson Mandela,*** *(Published by MacMillan in conjunction with The Nelson Mandela Foundation, London) © 2010.*

11. **Criminal Law 5th Edition,** *by Author CR Snyman (Published by Nexis Lexis Group, Durban, Johannesburg, Cape Town) © 2008.*

12. **Deliverance Workshop Manual,** *book by Pastor James Lottering, (Port Elizabeth, South Africa) © 2005.*

13. **Education in Prisons: Studying through Distance Learning,** *book by Emma Hughes (Published by Ashgate, California, USA) © 2012.*

14. **Emotional Healing,** *book by New Life Ministries, Dr Randall and Dr Rochelle Appel, (Goodwood, Cape Town, South Africa) © 2016.*

15. **Forensics, The Anatomy of Crime,** *book by Val Mc Dermid, (London, Great Britain), © 2014.*

16. **Grief Counselling and Grief Therapy, A Handbook for the Mental Health Practitioner,** *book by Author J. William Worden, Published by Routledge, London, UK © Third Edition 2001.*

17. **Grow in your Spiritual Life, book by** *Dr Hennie van Deventer, written for Nehemiah Bible Institute (Wellington, South Africa) © 2011.*

18. **Healing your Past, Releasing your Future,** *book by Frank Fabiano and Catherine Cahill-Fabiano, (Published by Sovereign World Ltd, Lancaster, England) © Second Edition 2016.*

19. **Homicide: A Forensic Psychology Casebook,** *book by Joan Swart and Lee Mellor (Published by CRC Press, Canada and California, USA) © 2017.*

20. **Introduction to Christian Education and Formation,** *book by Ronald T. Habermas (Published by Zondervan) © 2009.*

21. **Introduction to Psychology and Counselling, Christian Perspectives and Applications,** *Amazon online book by Paul D. Meier, Frank B. Minirth, Frank B. Wichern and Donald E. Ratcliff (Published by Baker Books) © Second Edition 2000.*

22. **Investigating Child Exploitation and Pornography: The Internet, Law and Forensic Science,** *book by Monique Ferraro and Eoghan Casey, (Published by Elsevier Academic Press, Burlington and California, USA) © 2005.*

23. ***Justice Denied, The Role of Forensic Science in the Miscarriage of Justice,*** *book by David Klatzow, (Zebra Press, Century City, Cape Town) © First edition 2014.*

24. ***Justice Not Silence, Churches Facing Sexual and Gender-Based Violence,*** *book by Ezra Chitando and Sophia Chirongoma, Published by Sun Press in conjunction with EFSA Institute for Theological and Interdisciplinary Research, Stellenbosch, Cape Town, SA© 2013.*

25. ***Kairos Prison Ministry Advanced Leadership and Mentoring Training,*** *book by Kevin Rosnover (FL, USA) © 2008.*

26. ***Law of Criminal Procedure and Evidence Casebook,*** *by Authors AM Sorgdrager, EJS Coertzen, JH Bezuidenthout, F Nel (Published by Butterworths, Durban) © 1994.*

27. ***Living Theology, Essays Presented to Dirk J. Smit,*** *Editors Len Hansen, Nico Koopman and Robert Vosloo (Published by Bible Media, Wellington, South Africa) © 2013.*

28. ***Managing High-Risk Offenders in the Community: A Psychological Approach,*** *book by Jacki Craissati (Published by Brunner-Routledge, Hove and New York, USA) © 2004.*

29. ***Mending a Shattered Heart, A Guide for Partners of sex Addicts, book by Stefanie Carnes Ph.D.*** *(Gentle Pass Press, Carefree, Arizona, USA) © Third print 2011.*

30. ***My Pledge: Committed to Change,*** *book by Val Hamann (Published by Biblecor, Bible Media, Wellington, Cape Town) © 2016.*

31. ***Necrophilia Forensic and Medico-Legal Aspects,*** *book by Anwil Aggrawal (Published by CRC Press, Florida, USA) © 2011.*

32. ***Pedophilia Empire: Satan, Sodomy and the Deep State,*** *book by Joachim Hagopian (Published by Kindle) © 2018.*

33. ***Perverts and Predators: The Making of sexual Offender Laws,*** *book by Laura J. Zilney and Lisa Anne Zilney (Published by Rowman and Littlefield Publishers Inc., Maryland, UK) © 2009.*

34. ***Prison Ministry Leadership Workshops for South Africa,*** *book by Val Hamann (Published by CLF Publishers, Wellington, Cape Town) © 2020.*

35. ***Prison Re-entry Programs: Penetrating the Black Box for Better Theory and Practise,*** *book written by Eric L. Grommon (Published by LFB Scholarly Publishing) © 2013.*

36. ***Professional Communication, How to deliver effective written and spoken messages,*** *Book by J. English, M. Fielding, E. Howard, N. van der Merwe (Lansdowne, Cape Town) © 2002.*

37. ***Psychology, The Science of Mind and Behaviour,*** *book by Michael Passer, Ronald Smith, Nigel Holt, Andy Bremmer, Ed Sutherland and Michael Vliek, (Published by McGraw-Hill Education, UK) © 2009.*

38. ***Psychoeducational Groups, Process and Practise,*** *book by Nina W. Brown, (New York, USA) © Third edition 2011.*

39. ***Reimagining Christian Education: Cultivating Transformative Approaches,*** *book by Johannes M. Leutz, Tony Dowden and Beverley Norsworthy (Published by Springer, Brisbane, Australia) © 2018.*

40. ***Religion and Social Development in Post-Apartheid South Africa, Perspectives for critical engagement,*** *book by Editors Ignatius Swart, Hermann Rocher, Sulina Green, Johannes Erasmus (African Sun Media, Stellenbosch South Africa) © 2010.*

41. ***Rethinking Rehabilitation: Why can't we reform our criminals?*** *Book by David Farabee (Published by American Enterprise Inst, Washington DC, USA) © 2005.*

42. ***Sex Offender Treatment: A case Study Approach to Issues and Interventions,*** *book by Garrett, Tanya Harkins, Leigh Wilcox and Daniel T (Published by Wiley Blackwell, West Sussex, UK) © 2015.*

43. ***Sixty ways to start up a Study Group and Keep it Going,*** *book by Lawrence O. Richards, (Published by Pyranee Books, Zondervan, Grand Rapids, Michigan, USA) © 1973.*

44. ***Social Intelligence, The New Science of Human Relationships***, *book by Daniel Coleman (Published by Hutchinson, London, UK) © 2006.*

45. ***Social Psychology,*** *book by Robert A. Baron, Nyla R. Branscombe and Donn Byrne, (Published by Pearson Education International) Twelfth Edition © 2009.*

46. ***Spiritual Growth and Spiritual Formation,*** *book by New Life Ministries, Dr Randall and Dr Rochelle Appel, (Goodwood, Cape Town, South Africa) © 2016.*

47. ***The Perversion of Youth: Controversies in the Assessment and Treatment of Juvenile Sex offenders,*** *Amazon online book by Frank C. Dicataldo (Published by New York University, London and New York) © 2009.*

48. ***The Suicide and Homicide Risk Assessment and Prevention: Treatment Planner,*** *Amazon online book by Arthur E. Jongsma Jnr. And Jack Klott (Published by John Wiley & Sons Inc. New Jersey, USA) © 2004.*

49. ***Theories of Personality,*** *book by Duane P. Schultz and Sydney Ellen Schultz, (USA) © International Edition 2013.*

50. ***Training Disciple Makers,*** *book by Dr Hennie van Deventer, written for Nehemiah Bible Institute (Wellington, South Africa) © 2013.*

51. ***Understanding Necrophilia, 1ˢᵗ Edition,*** *book by Lee Melor, Anwil Aggrawal and Eric Hickey (Published by Cognella Academic Publishing, USA) © 2017.*

52. ***War within Man, A Psychological Enquiry into the Roots of Destructiveness,*** *book by Erich Fromm, (Published by Cambridge, Massachusetts, USA) © 1963.*

53. *Good news Bible, © 1977* ***(GNB: 1977)*** *& The Holy Bible King James Version, California* ***(KJV: 1976).***

ii. Website references and journals, dates of information downloaded:

1. ***Education Opportunities in Prison are Key to Reducing Crime,*** *by Author Kathleen Bender www.americanprogress.org © March 2018 – Retrieved March 2021.*

2. ***Education in Prison: A basic right and essential tool,*** *by Author Hugo Rangel Torino and Marc de Maeyer (Published International Review of Education) https://link.springer.com/article/10.1007/s11159-019-09809-x © October 2019 – Retrieved March 2021.*

3. ***Education Programmes for Prison Inmates: Rewards for Offences or Hope for a Better Life?*** *By Author Kofi Poku Quan-Baffor and Britta E. Zawada (Published by Unisa) © 2012, Retrieved March 2021.*

4. ***Locked Up and Locked Out: An Educational Perspective on the US Prison Population, Policy Information Report,*** *by Authors Richard J. Coley and Paul E. Barton (Published by Educational testing Service) © February 2006 – Retrieved March 2021.*

5. ***The State of South African Prisons,*** *by Author Regan Jules-Macquet (Published by NICRO Education Series) http://press.nicro.org.za/images/PDF/Public-Education-Paper-The-State-of-South-African-Prisons-2014.pdf © Edition 1, 2014 PDF – Retrieved February 2021.*

iii. Interviews and meetings

(See Annexure A for questions posed to the following prison ministry leaders):

A. **Mrs Mercial Adonis, Nehemiah Bible Institute Prison Ministry Division, Bible Media Group (NPO),** working with correspondence educational programs with offenders and ex-offenders and pastoral care counselling for offenders, via correspondence country-wide and ex-offenders in the Boland area. Interview date: 29 April 2021 in Malmesbury. See www.nehemiah.co.za

B. **Pastor Maxwell Benjamin, Prison Ministry Leader,** prison ministry amongst hard-edged gangsters only, Department of Correctional Services, Drakenstien Prison, Boland, Western Cape. Interview date: 13 April 2021 in Paarl.

C. **Ms Ronelle Hendricks, Prison Ministry Leader, Kairos Prison Ministry International,** mentors offenders for reintegration into society, reducing recidivism. Interview date: 13 April 2021 via Skype.

D. **Mr Cyril Naicker, Chief Executive of Fashion Revolution,** works in the fashion industry, integrating ministry and ethical fashion, assisting with job creation of beading work for fashion garments, for ex-offenders and promotes the importance of prison ministry education to rehabilitate offenders, teaching them life skills and other Christian programs, for them to know that God cares about their lives. He claims that helping ex-offenders with employment opportunities, reduces recidivism, as he has witnessed it first-hand. Interview date: 10 March 2021 in Cape Town.

E. **Mr Ulrich Eldrid Lottering, Managing Director of Networking for Christ South Africa (NFCSA, NPO),** working with educational programs with offenders and ex-offenders, victims of crime, development skills for employment opportunities for ex-offenders, drug rehabilitation, life skills, other ex-inmate aftercare services. (NFCSA) Offers counselling at Police Stations for victims of Gender Based Violence. Interview date: 5 April 2021 in Wellington. See www.nfcsa.org.za

F. **Mark Slessenger, Managing Director of The Message Trust (NPO),** works with ex-offenders teaching them work and entrepreneurial skills in Cape Town, South Africa. Interview date: 12 November 2021.

G. **Six Pastors,** five wish to remain anonymous, sixth Ps Maxwell Benjamin (Paarl) Interview dates: March/April/May 2021 in Wellington, Malmesbury and Durbanville.

H. **Three offenders,** names protected for privacy and prison protocols. Interview date: 1 May 2021 at Allandale Correctional Centre and 12 May 2021 at Drakenstein Correctional Centre, in Paarl.

About the Author

Dr. Rev. Val Hamann (Ph.D.) was born in Germiston, South Africa in June 1967 and lives in Wellington, Cape Town, she relocated in 2002. She started facilitating small groups in 2010 and has been actively involved in ministry since.

Val devotes much of her spare time to writing Christian based life skills books for prisoners and Christian women's healing programs. An excellent all-rounder, Val obtained her Bachelors and Bachelor Honours in Ministry, Master's Degree in Christian Education and Doctorate in Counselling.

Val is an ordained pastor who loves to experience hurting people heal. She conducts motivational speaking, group counselling at prisons and churches, runs women's groups and camps, as well as positively impacts the youth at community rallies.

Val is a member of the AFM Church, Protea Center Paarl. She volunteers through Networking for Christ SA (NPO) facilitating, counselling, lecturing college students and running women's healing programs for community members and victims of crime.

Val received honorary awards for personal development and community development in 2021.

Val enjoys hearing from her readers, please contact her via post P O Box 5, Wellington, South Africa 7655, or via email valeriehamann@gmail.com

Other books written by the same author

The lessons in **Socially Acceptable** will equip prisoners with knowledge of social skills inside and outside prison, specifically those who did not have the advantage of attending school. The purpose of this book is to guide you as a human being to get to know yourself and others by having respect for different levels of relationships and by knowing your responsibility and rights as part of a social structure. Available in English, Afrikaans and Xhosa. **Published by Bible Media.**

The Only Way Out is a Bible study aimed at prisoners and can be used by individuals or Bible study groups. These lessons have been designed to apply to your daily life, so that you can come to know the God of love who stretches out his hand to you, his child, today to give you the only way out. It deals with lies, dealing with divorce and death of family members while in prison, resisting temptations to belong to gangs, dealing with anger, hurt, forgiveness, love and avoiding re-offending. Available in English and Xhosa. **Published by Bible Media.**

Liberty in Captivity is a program that is aimed at prisoners for individual or group Bible study. It is written in a clear language, is short and the lay out is simple. These lessons have been designed to apply to your daily life, to come to know that God of love stretches his hand out to you, his child, today. Available in English, Afrikaans and Xhosa. **Published by Bible Media.**

Your Life: Your Choice is a program aimed at prisoners teaching them life skills, making better choices and realising the ripple effect of their crimes. Available in English and Xhosa. **Published by Bible Media.**

My pledge: Committed to Change is aimed at prisoner's social integration, changing their behaviour patterns to making better choices, to be a better man for God, community and family. Every inmate is worth more than their last day. Available in English and Xhosa. **Published by Bible Media.**

Masquerade: What Mask Are You Hiding Behind? What expression do others see on our faces when they look at us? Do our faces depict the true condition of our hearts, our circumstances, our emotions and our past experiences? What are we hiding? If we say that Jesus lives inside of us, can others see it in us and through us? What would happen if we show our true self to the world? Are you brave enough to embark on this journey to shed your mask? How do we get to the point of just being ourselves and being who God created us to be? Available in English, Afrikaans and Xhosa. **Published by Bible Media.**

South African Prison Ministry Leadership Workshop has a facilitator manual and participant's workbook, tailored to South African prison requirements and designed to train teams of people interested in conducting or starting up a prison ministry in their local towns. Available in English. **Published by CLF Publishers.**

Family Preservation Series - Love and sex as God designed it, Marriage as God designed it, Divorce recovery intervention program: A CPD program for ex-offenders. Available in English. **Published by: Bible Media, Biblekor.**

The books published by Bible Media for prison ministry, have 96%+ footprint success in SA prisons.

Heart Sparks Women's Healing Program has a facilitator manual and participant's workbook, designed for four Saturdays in a row, or a long weekend Christian women's camp. It deals with challenges women face and has exciting interactive projects, that promote healing and wholeness from past traumatic events. Available in English. **Self-Published.**

Cake with the King has a facilitator manual and workbook, an addendum to **Heart Sparks**, designed for women's Christian groups or long weekend camps. It deals with challenges women face and has exciting interactive projects, that promote healing and wholeness from past traumatic events and a lot of cake baking and tasting! **Self-Published.**

Crushing the excuse for abuse! This is a comprehensive **Gender Based Violence and Victim Empowerment Program (GBV & VE)** with a facilitator manual and workbook assisting perpetrators and victims of various forms of abuse. **Funded by Department of Social Development** for community development. Available in English and Afrikaans. Published by Networking for Christ NPO. **Published by NFC (SA).**